(Mention Your Request Here)
The Church's Most Powerful Novenas

Michael Dubruiel

Our Sunday Visitor Publishing Division
Our Sunday Visitor, Inc.
Huntington, Indiana 46750

ISBN: 0-87973-341-1
LCCCN: 99-75031

Cover design by Tyler Ottinger
PRINTED IN THE UNITED STATES OF AMERICA

For my mother, Barbara Dubruiel, who took the time not only to read this book but also to pray it. May everyone else who picks it up follow her example.

Table of Contents

Foreword by Father Benedict J. Groeschel, C.F.R. _____ 7

Introduction _____ 15

Acknowledgments _____ 23

PART 1: NOVENAS TO JESUS

1 / Infant Jesus of Prague _____ 28

2 / Sacred Heart of Jesus _____ 36

3 / Divine Mercy _____ 45

PART 2: NOVENA TO THE HOLY SPIRIT

4 / St. Maximilian Kolbe _____ 62

PART 3: NOVENAS TO THE BLESSED VIRGIN MARY

5 / The Immaculate Conception _____ 82

6 / Our Lady of La Leche _____ 89

7 / Our Lady of the Miraculous Medal _____ 93

8 / Our Lady of Monte Cassino _____ 99

9 / Our Lady of Mount Carmel _____ 104

10 / Our Lady of Perpetual Help _____ 113

11 / Our Lady of Prompt Succor _____ 120

12 / Our Lady of the Snows _____ 125

PART 4: NOVENAS TO THE RELATIVES OF JESUS

13 / St. Ann _____ 130

14 / St. Joseph _____ 136

15 / St. Jude _____ 155

Part 5: Novenas to Particular Saints

16 / St. Anthony of Padua _____ 162

17 / St. Gerard Majella _____ 168

18 / St. Peregrine _____ 179

19 / St. Rita of Cascia _____ 191

20 / St. Thérèse of Lisieux _____ 198

Part 6: Novenas to American Saints

21 / North American Martyrs _____ 204

22 / St. Elizabeth Ann Seton _____ 211

23 / St. Frances Xavier Cabrini _____ 217

24 / St. John Neumann _____ 222

25 / Blessed Katharine Drexel _____ 233

Part 7: Novena for the Holy Souls

26 / St. Odilo _____ 240

Prayers Common to Novenas _____ 252

Foreword

Novenas: A Comeback

As I was working on this foreword during a pilgrimage to Lourdes, someone asked me what I was writing about. When I answered, "Novenas," the response was, "Are they making a comeback?" That got me thinking. What is making a comeback is personal prayer or, as it is sometimes called, "private prayer." Despite the direct advice of Our Lord (Matthew 6:4-6) that when we pray we should go into our room and shut the door and pray to Our Father in secret, private prayer had become a bit of a "no-no" in recent decades — another aspect of the decline of Catholicism. This particular decline began innocently enough with the emphasis on liturgical prayer over private prayer. If there was any imbalance in favor of private prayer it was because most people only minimally participated in liturgical prayer. Recall the eighteen-minute Mass in what was euphemistically called Latin and you will know why the faithful didn't participate. Soon, liturgical participation tended to be all-consuming and frequently was devoid of any expression of inner involvement. Solemn Latin hymns, which invited you to prayer and recollection even if you did not know what the words exactly meant, gave place to songs, some of which sounded as if they were written by Gilbert and Sullivan and others by Spike Jones.

In reaction, an interest in totally private and unstructured meditation came to fill a void; but often this was merely a process of psychological recollection rather than the experience of private prayer and devotion. The Charismatic experience also came to fill the void left by the complete banishment of devotional prayer, private and public, from parish life. The Catholic Charismatic experience offered a whole range of devotional prayer — liturgical and private, including praise, thanksgiving, repentance, and intercession. But the enthusiasm of this movement was not everybody's "cup of devotion."

To take the place of devotional prayer, including Eucharistic devotion, to the personal presence of Christ and to replace popular novenas, a sort of Protestant service called the "Bible vigil" was contrived with good will but with no appreciation of devotion at all. Mercifully, this contrivance was so reminiscent of the boring services held on Wednesday night at the local evangelical tabernacle that it died a quick death. Most younger Catholics have at least heard of novenas, but none of them know what a Bible vigil is.

The incredible and growing popularity of the Eucharistic Holy Hour, in the face of stiff opposition, signals the beginning of a new era in Catholic religious life. As a psychologist interested in things spiritual, I can only offer grateful thanks to the Lord because the religious experience of many Catholics was beginning to resemble a state of chronic anemia and the resultant "atrophication" of members of the Church started to look like a situation best described as "chronic religious leukemia." The voice of the people of God is being heard at last over the whirl of the duplicating machines.

Younger Catholics, despite a generally dreadful religious education, are looking for an integrated expression of faith — mind, heart, body, and soul with all their needs expressed. Scripture recently, so much the province of an extreme rationalistic and intellectualized approach, is now beginning to be studied for what it has to say to the individual. In Europe, especially in France, but spreading everywhere, there is a youthful enthusiasm that joins reverential liturgical ceremonies filled with an awareness of the Eucharistic presence, with Scripture and personal prayer, what we used to call Eucharistic devotions. Joined to this is contemporary religious music inspired by the classical forms of the past. As I write these lines, my mind is filled with the magnificent music of the young people of the Jerusalem community whom I heard singing in a French cathedral yesterday.

With all this going on, it is no surprise at all to learn that novenas are coming back too. The task now is to make sure that they return intelligently — that is, in a way that is consistent with Scripture and good theology. Hopefully, this book will help to fill that need.

A Bit of History

Novenas are prayers of devotion that are offered for nine days or over some other period of time with a factor of nine. They had their origin in ancient Rome as times of prayer for the dead over a nine-day period. They were essentially prayers of mourning and commendation of the soul to the mercy of God. Many times I have participated in this kind of novena held by the Puerto Rican people after the death of a dear one.

In the early Middle Ages, novenas became ways of preparing for great liturgical events, especially Christmas. One novena became linked to the antiphons of Vespers, which begin with the vocative "O" nine days before the celebration of Christ's birth. We recognize this custom from the Advent hymn "O Come, O Come, Emmanuel," which in fact is the first antiphon of this novena.

This novena may have been related in people's minds to the nine months that the infant Savior remained in his mother's womb. For this reason, novenas began to be associated with Our Lady, particularly in France and Spain. A bit later, the novena became associated with the nine days from Ascension to Pentecost. This kind of prayer had the advantage of a strong scriptural foundation. Indeed, the Apostles did, without knowing the name, make a novena of prayer while waiting for the Holy Spirit.

Since Our Lord himself counseled persistent and repetitive prayer in the parables of the Importunate Neighbor (Luke 11:5-9) and the Unjust Judge (Luke 18:1-7), it became obvious that the novena could be used for intercession, asking the Lord for what one needs. Novenas could also be an act of penance and sometimes imposed, one assumes, for fairly serious sins on the occasion of the sacrament of reconciliation.

If your memory goes back before Vatican II, you will recall that every respectable parish had its perpetual or ongoing novena. These were in honor of the Sacred Heart of Jesus Christ under some title or they were devotions to Mary as Our Lady of Perpetual Help (originally a devotion of the Eastern churches) or of Our Lady of the Miraculous Medal or even Our Lady of Sorrows. Various saints had their own novenas, usually preceding their feast days; but St. Anthony was so popular that he might find himself bombarded by prayer on a weekly basis throughout the year.

Parish novenas had several things in common — popular hymns and prayers in the vernacular, a devotional sermon, followed by Benediction of the Blessed Sacrament. They were expressions of popular piety that were rather rigidly controlled. The hymns and the prayers represented the best examples of the folk religion and piety that most of our ancestors had packed into their shabby baggage as they came as immigrants through the golden door of Ellis Island. In the beautiful and moving museum of the old immigration station of Ellis Island there is a remarkable display of several religious articles of the immigrants — Jewish prayer stoles, Lutheran Bibles, and, of course, rosaries and novena books.

Novenas were such a popular form of Catholic devotion because the liturgy remained largely locked up in silent Latin and was simply an obligation to those people who were not inclined to use missals. Most people, in fact, did not use or even own a missal. Many who sat passively at the liturgy enthusiastically sang and prayed at the novena. In the early 1940s, when I first served as an altar boy at the novenas to Our Lady, one of my crusty Irish neighbors asked me if I was on my way to that Protestant service. He saw it as Protestant because it was in the vernacular and it was popular. He was probably a bit suspicious too, because unlike Mass you could enjoy a novena.

There Are Always Problems

Like all things, novenas can have their problems. They can be overly sentimental or, on the other hand, to control this tendency the prayers may be very theological to keep them from being sentimental. The Miraculous Medal Novena had it all — succinct, scriptural, theological, written in English a bit more polished than most of us ordinarily spoke and with a beautiful benediction at the end, and then, unfortunately, an over-sentimental hymn with very poor theology — "Good Night, Sweet Jesus." This was sung only by candlelight in the darkened church. But don't laugh. Later in the course of teaching a couple of thousand adults, then in their forties and fifties, I discovered that the most moving religious experience that the largest number remembered was singing this hymn by candlelight.

Another problem of novenas is that they can give rise to superstition, that is, things people believe because they need to believe them. My impression is that modern life is filled with far more medical, scientific, and political superstitions than religious ones. People believe in politicians who are known liars and take remedies that no scientific evidence supports and engage in experiences of psychotherapy of the most doubtful benefit. Religion is probably one area of life that has fewer superstitions than others because at least religious people are on the watch for superstition.

The simple fact is that no prayer — whether it be a novena or anything else — can change the mind of God because he has no change in him at all. But, as we have noted, Christ tells us in the parables to pray and suggests we importune the Lord like the widow who harried the unjust judge. "Ask and you shall receive, seek and you shall find, knock and it shall be opened unto you" (Luke 11:9).

Novenas are nothing more or less than forms of insistent prayer. God does not need nine prayers or even one prayer to know what we really need, but mysteriously Christ tells us to pray incessantly and assures us that God will give his Holy Spirit to those who ask him. He also tells us that he will provide what we really need and not merely what we simply want. Otherwise, we poor creatures would ruin the world. Can you imagine the complete disaster if we all got what we asked for?

It is worth mentioning that a particularly annoying form of superstition was associated with novenas in the past. This is the "chain novena" often proposed by letter and now by e-mail. Some devout soul is misled into thinking a certain prayer is said by nine people and each engage nine other people so that X, Y, or Z will happen. This is superstition, and such letters should be quietly destroyed or deleted and perhaps the good soul who wrote them originally should be kindly warned that this is a form of superstition and forbidden by the Church.

Novenas have always been popular with the poor — those very same people who followed Jesus around. After a half century of working with them, I know that the poor know how to pray on average better than the rest of us. I can't resist ending this foreword with a story. I knew of a very wonderful, generous old lady from the Caribbean — a Protestant who cared for her invalid husband for years until he died. They lived in the same apartment in Harlem for more than fifty years. And after her husband died, she wanted to fix her apartment up a bit, since it had been a sickroom for so long a time. The widow calculated that she needed twelve hundred dollars, which was a respectable sum twenty-five years ago. She needed to paint the rooms and get some decent furniture. Her humble Catholic friend, Rosita, told her about novenas and suggested that together they should make one to the Blessed Virgin Mary. Mrs. Mack decided she could fit this in with her Protestant convictions and on the ninth night of the novena she had a very vivid dream of seeing her husband on the sidewalk five stories below. He called up to her, "Hey, Maw, play the number." The number was the series 4, 5, and 6, a series that Jimmy had unsuccessfully played with the bookie for years because it paid double. Mrs. Mack was not a gambling woman at all, but she felt she had no choice. She sent a neighbor's son around the corner with two dollars to the bookie. In the afternoon, he returned with twelve hundred dollars on the nose.

This account may make you feel uneasy. Don't blame me. Cross my heart — it's true. Mrs. Mack died with the sacraments of the Catholic Church and deep devotion to the Blessed Virgin Mary. If it doesn't make sense to you, then read over the words of Our Lord (Luke 11:11-13):

> What father among you, if his son asks for a fish, will instead of a fish give him a serpent; or if he asks for an egg, will give him a scorpion? If you then, who are evil, know how to give good gifts to your children, how much more will the heavenly Father give the Holy Spirit to those who ask him!

And don't complain to me. I made a lot of novenas in my youth and in later years I usually just put myself confidently into the hands of Jesus calling upon his mother who is also mine. I didn't get everything I asked for or even everything I felt I needed. But looking back over six decades of insistent, if not devout, prayer, I can unhesitatingly say "Amen" to the words of the Gospel: "Ask and you shall receive, seek and you shall find, knock and it shall be opened to you" (Luke 11:9).

FATHER BENEDICT J. GROESCHEL, C.F.R.

Introduction

Jacob was fleeing for his life, but at the point of exhaustion he could go no further. Now under the cover of darkness he found a spot where he could rest for the night. Under the expansive desert sky, he placed a rock for a pillow under his head. Perhaps he did this so he would not sleep too deeply, but soon sleep came. Before long, his imagination awakened him and he dreamed of a staircase that went from the rock his head rested upon to the throne of God in heaven. Angels of God were descending and ascending the staircase.

In the dream, God assured Jacob of his presence and protection. When he awoke, Jacob poured oil over the rock that had been both a source of rest and the first step to knowledge of God's love. He consecrated the place a shrine, calling it Bethel, or "House of God."

Thus begins the history of shrines, places set aside to commemorate religious experiences and dedicated to the worship of God. A recent Vatican document defines a shrine as "a church or other sacred place to which the faithful make pilgrimages for a particular religious reason, with the approval of the local Ordinary" (*The Shrine: Memory, Presence and Prophecy of the Living God*, Pontifical Council for the Pastoral Care of Migrants and Itinerant People, May 1999, no. 1). Shrines arise one stone at a time, built on the faith experiences of individuals like Jacob, the great patriarch in the Book of Genesis, until they tower over the landscape and beckon others to come and be still so that they, too, might know the Lord.

Jesus identified himself with the staircase in Jacob's vision when he told Nathaniel in the Gospel of John that he would see "heaven open and the angels of God ascending and descending *on* the Son of Man" (my emphasis). Jesus is the staircase that leads from every shrine to the very presence of God.

"The deepest meaning of every shrine is to serve as a reminder in faith of the salvific work of the Lord" (*The Shrine: Memory, Presence and Prophecy of the Living God*, no. 4).

Shrines remind us that God has first loved us, without any merit on our part. The very response that we make to God's love is itself a gift of grace from God. "This conviction is further expressed in the shrine through the specific message connected with it, whether in regard to the mysteries of the life of Jesus Christ, in regard to one of the titles of Mary, 'who shines forth to the whole community of the elect as a model of virtues,' or in regard to the individual saints whose memory proclaims the 'wonderful works of Christ in his servants' " (*The Shrine: Memory, Presence and Prophecy of the Living God*, no. 6).

Shrines have come into existence in the United States since the first moment that a Christian set foot on its shores, that is, when Mass was celebrated in St. Augustine, Florida, on September 8, 1565, by Father Francisco López de Mendoza Grajales. Each shrine points to a particular way that individuals have found a way to encounter Christ and to deepen their relationship with God.

This book contains novena prayers that are used at shrines in the United States. The shrines stand as living monuments to the efficacy of the prayers that have been prayed in them. Those who have donated their labor and wealth in thanksgiving to God for prayers answered have built the shrines and invoked the prayers contained herein.

A novena is a challenging form of prayer. Whereas the recitation of the prayer or a set of prayers may be easy, doing it for nine consecutive days is not. Our lives are crowded and it is often easy to let the prayer pass. I like to think of the practice of praying a novena as setting the groundwork for a life of prayer. Consider the possible benefits of praying a novena besides the actual requests that one mentions in them.

First, you develop the habit of praying daily. Our lives are filled with ritual from the time we get up in the morning: the route we take to work and home again, how we spend our evenings, and the usual time we go to bed. Day in and out the pattern is repeated. Is prayer a part of that daily routine? Praying a novena for nine consecutive days can set a pattern of prayer in our lives that can create a daily habit of prayer.

Second, praying a novena reinforces a sense that God is our Father and that God loves us. Well-meaning people have done a very good job of spreading a false gospel that good Christians shouldn't ask God for anything, that we shouldn't be seeking favors from the Father. This is sad and clearly not in keeping with the teaching of the Gospel, where Jesus asks, "What do you want me to do for you?" (Mark 10:51).

In the *Spiritual Exercises* of St. Ignatius of Loyola the founder of the Jesuits instructed his retreatants to begin every period of prayer by imploring God for a particular grace that they wished to receive as a result of the prayer. At the very end of his *Exercises* Ignatius instructs the retreatant to make what he calls a "Contemplation to Attain Divine Love." This reflection is made by contemplating how lovers enjoy giving gifts to their beloved. Ignatius has the retreatant reflect that if God loves us, certainly he must also give us gifts. The retreatant then reflects on what gifts God has given to them personally in their lifetime. Praying intently for nine days can deepen our communion with God and enliven our hope that God truly cares for us.

A third benefit is the involvement of others in our prayer life. While the Second Vatican Council sought to renew a sense of the communal nature of prayer, some of the more zealous sought to achieve this by erasing one aspect of Catholicism where the sense of communal prayer was already a lived reality: the involvement of the Church victorious — the saints.

Recently while I was visiting an Eastern Orthodox Church, the beauty and the symbolism of the iconostasis struck me. An iconostasis is a wall of icons (consisting of painted images of God, the Blessed Virgin, and the saints) that separates the sanctuary from the nave of the church. In Orthodox churches the walls are covered with icons as a testament that when we on earth gather in prayer we do not pray alone, but are joined by all of those who have gone before us and are now in heaven.

The next day, while I was at Mass in an inner-city church in Detroit, Michigan, I was struck by the statues of the saints (which, in the post-Vatican II Church, are a rarity) and how much they resembled the iconostasis of the Orthodox Church, except ours were three-dimensional. Obviously, the presence of the saints in both churches is a testament that God wants all of us to pray for one another, and that does not stop when our earthly life is over.

All prayer is directed ultimately to God the Father, Son, and Holy Spirit, and as much as we honor the saints by inviting them to pray with us, God is still the object of our worship and praise. Many of the shrines contained in this book have images of the saints' lives artistically presented in stained-glass windows. This reminds me of the story of a little girl who one day pointed to such a window in a church and asked her mother what it was.

"They are saints," her mother replied.

It happened that the next day the child was attending religion class in her school and the subject of the lesson was saints. "Does anyone know what a saint is?" the teacher asked.

The little girl anxiously raised her hand along with several other classmates. The teacher, recognizing her, pointed and said, "Yes, Rachel?"

"Saints are people the light shines through," was the little girl's response.

I cannot think of a better theological description of saints. They are people who have allowed the light of Christ to shine through in their lives. Their focus is God, and in honoring them we can only draw closer to God.

In the stories of the devotions in this book I have sought to give the traditional story without apology. I know there are those who question the veracity of some of these tales, but in some of their reasoning they betray a subtle skepticism of anything miraculous. I have tried to recount the stories as most of them have traditionally been passed on. If some make you smile, that is fine; but you might take the time to reflect on what lesson might be learned if in fact the story is not true but merely a parable. What will seem incredulous to one often reveals how limited we feel God is in the created world in which we live.

I have converted some of the novenas in this book from their communal form, where a presider and congregation have parts, to a form that allows each of the prayers to be prayed individually. How each individual uses them is a matter of personal taste; some will find that prayers to a particular devotion fit the need of the present moment, while others may seek to honor a particular devotion in conjunction with a feast day connected with it.

All prayer is efficacious, because God is ever faithful, but the wording of these prayers stands as a testimony of people who, we might say, "knew how to talk to God." In making their words ours, we can only hope to learn that particular art. Jesus taught his disciples how to pray by teaching them the Our Father; so, too, in these prayers we have a lesson taught by those who have been faithful in seeking the kingdom of God first and have been rewarded for it.

I have included a section in the book that I've entitled "Prayers Common to Novenas," which includes prayers that are used in a number of the novenas in this work. Please refer to this section as needed.

In the descriptions of the shrines I have relied on my memory and the help of the various individuals affiliated with the shrines included in the book. All errors that might be included are my fault alone. I have visited most of them personally, not as a tourist but as a pilgrim. I invite you to do the same on your journeys. As one ventures into these hallowed spots, one can almost tangibly feel the presence of God lingering over the structures, no doubt the result of the countless prayers and conversions that have occurred within their walls. As the Vatican document on shrines says, "One enters a shrine with a spirit of adoration" (*The Shrine: Memory, Presence and Prophecy of the Living God*, no. 6).

Many of the shrines in this book have websites. If you have access to the Internet you can pilgrimage to these sites by merely entering the website address included in the contact information of every shrine. Some shrines have places for you to enter prayer petitions so that as you make a novena your petitions can be placed at the altar of the shrine. A few places also offer devotional material attached to the shrine that you can obtain free of charge. It is well worth your while to visit these sites.

Finally, a personal note. I have written my portion of this book as an act of thanksgiving to God for the many prayers that have been answered throughout my life. I am tempted to label God's care for me as evidence of his great sense of humor. At one time or another I have prayed most of the novenas in this book and God has never *not* answered the petitions — albeit in ways that I could never have envisioned.

The most recent example involved a novena that I made to the Little Flower, St. Thérèse of Lisieux. A friend had told me that when you pray a novena to St. Thérèse, she would send you flowers as evidence that she is indeed praying for you. I smiled rather condescendingly at the notion, which I felt bordered on superstition, but began the novena anyway with no expectation of a visit from the florist.

The next day I received an ad in the mail for rosebushes. I took one look at it, smiled, and threw it in the trash wondering how I had gotten on a gardening mailing list, since gardening is not one of my personal interests. The next day I received the same advertisement again; this time I pondered it awhile, wondering, but finally flung it in the same direction as its predecessor. A week later I received a holy card of St. Thérèse surrounded by roses from someone that I had not heard from in five years. I kept this.

I had been praying about a career change, having tired of teaching high-school students, and it seemed to be answered miraculously when I was hired to co-write a screenplay for a major television network. Before long, I moved out to California, and the future looked very bright. But then in the midst of all the apparent success, everything fell apart, and I remember feeling duped by God and let down because of my faith. On the very day that I prepared to head back East, I was given an oil painting as a gift; it was of St. Thérèse holding a crucifix and a bouquet of roses. Somehow I knew that God was still on my side and that everything would turn out okay.

It seems that it has. I hope that you will find this book informative about the various devotions and shrines. I hope that it will inspire you to step out in faith and to pray the prayers included between these covers, and above all I pray that you will know that God loves you.

When Jesus ascended into heaven, he told his Apostles to stay where they were in Jerusalem and to "wait for the gift" that the Father had promised: the Holy Spirit. The Apostles did as the Lord commanded them. "They all joined together constantly in prayer, along with the women and Mary the mother of Jesus, and with his brothers" (Acts 1:14). Nine days passed, during which time they waited in faith and continued to pray. They received the gift of the Holy Spirit as had been promised. May we all have a share in their faith and act on it in our lives as we pray these novenas and "mention our requests" with faith and trust in God.

Acknowledgments

The genesis of this title — *(Mention Your Request Here)* — came about one day while my fellow acquisitions editor, Jackie Lindsey, and I were discussing the idea of doing a novena book. As we threw ideas around, it struck me that collecting popular novenas used at shrines around the country would make a great novena book. I convinced Greg Erlandson, the editor in chief of Our Sunday Visitor, to let me take on the project. He agreed, and you now hold in your hands the result.

The completion of this project would have been impossible if it were not for the cooperation of the individuals connected in one way or another with the shrines mentioned in this work. I would like to thank all these individuals for their enthusiastic participation in this project and encourage you to visit the shrines with which they are affiliated either as a pilgrim or in the case of some as a cyber-guest. The images and novena prayers included in this book appear through the graciousness of the people connected with the following shrines:

• Infant Jesus of Prague — The National Shrine of the Infant Jesus of Prague, Prague, Oklahoma

• Sacred Heart of Jesus — National Shrine of the Sacred Heart, Harleigh, Pennsylvania

• Divine Mercy — Congregation of Marians of the Immaculate Conception, Stockbridge, Massachusetts

• Holy Spirit — Marytown/Kolbe Shrine, Libertyville, Illinois

• Immaculate Conception — Basilica of the National Shrine of the Immaculate Conception, Washington, D.C.

• Our Lady of La Leche — Shrine of Our Lady of La Leche, St. Augustine, Florida

- Our Lady of the Miraculous Medal — Association of the Miraculous Medal, Perryville, Missouri
- Our Lady of Monte Cassino — St. Meinrad Archabbey, St. Meinrad, Indiana
- Our Lady of Mount Carmel — National Shrine of Our Lady of Mount Carmel, Middletown, New York
- Our Lady of Perpetual Help — Mission Church, Boston, Massachusetts
- Our Lady of Prompt Succor — Ursuline Community of New Orleans, Louisiana
- Our Lady of the Snows — Missionary Oblates at the National Shrine of Our Lady of the Snows, Belleville, Illinois
- St. Ann — Basilica of the National Shrine of St. Ann, Scranton, Pennsylvania
- St. Joseph — Oblates of St. Joseph, Santa Cruz, California
- St. Jude — St. Jude Shrine, Baltimore, Maryland; also St. Jude League, Chicago, Illinois
- St. Anthony — St. Anthony Shrine, Cincinnati, Ohio
- St. Gerard — National Shrine of St. Gerard Majella, Newark, New Jersey
- St. Peregrine — The Grotto, Portland, Oregon
- St. Rita — National Shrine of St. Rita of Cascia, Philadelphia, Pennsylvania
- St. Thérèse — Society of the Little Flower, Darien, Illinois
- North American Martyrs — Shrine of Our Lady of Martyrs, Auriesville, New York
- St. Elizabeth Ann Seton — National Shrine of St. Elizabeth Ann Seton, Emmitsburg, Maryland
- St. Frances Cabrini — National Shrine of St. Frances Xavier Cabrini, Chicago, Illinois

- St. John Neumann — National Shrine of St. John Neumann, Philadelphia, Pennsylvania
- Blessed Katharine Drexel — Sisters of the Blessed Sacrament, Bensalem, Pennsylvania
- All Souls (photo) — St. Odilo's, Berwyn, Illinois
- All Souls (novena prayer) — Josephite Fathers and Brothers, Baltimore, Maryland

Many thanks to each!

Part 1

Novenas to Jesus

"Whatever you ask in my name, I will do it,
that the Father may be glorified in the Son; if
you ask anything in my name, I will do it."

JOHN 14:13-14

CHAPTER 1
Infant Jesus of Prague

"The more you honor me,
the more I will bless you."

History of the Devotion

The image of the Infant Jesus of Prague originates from Spain, where a copy of a similar wooden statue was commissioned and, in 1556, given as a wedding gift to María Manriquez de Lara, the bride of a Czech nobleman, Lord Vratislav of Pernstyn. Before her death, María bequeathed the

Holy Infant statue to her daughter Polyxena, wife of Prince Zdenek Adalbert Lobkowitz. In 1628, the aged Princess Polyxena presented the statue to the friars of the Carmel of Prague, where it was placed in their chapel situated near the Church of Our Lady of Victories in Prague.

In 1631, Saxons invaded Prague and plundered the Carmelite monastery. The statue of the Infant of Prague was discarded in a trash pile behind the high altar of the church. In 1637, after the Saxons had left, Father Cyril of the Mother of God found the statue.

The statue was badly damaged; both arms of the infant had been broken off. It was cloaked in a dirty blue dress. The cult of dressing the statue goes back to this time.

Placing the image upright and reverencing it, Father Cyril was shocked when the image spoke to him saying, "Have pity on me, and I will have pity on you. Give me my hands, and I will give you peace. The more you honor me, the more I will bless you."

Inspired by the words of the Infant Jesus to him, Father Cyril set out to find a benefactor to cover the costs of the repairs necessary for the restoration of the image. After many failed attempts, Father Cyril finally located a Prague citizen who not only donated money for the restoration of the statue but also for the building of a chapel in which the statue of the Infant of Prague would be enshrined.

In 1655, the bishop of Prague crowned the statue on the Feast of the Ascension. Since that time devotion to the Infant Jesus of Prague has spread throughout the world.

When communist power fell in Eastern Europe in the 1980s, American anchorman Dan Rather broadcast the *CBS Evening News* from in front of the altar where the Infant of Prague statue is enshrined and pointed to it as a sign of the faith of the people of Prague.

Novena to the Infant Jesus of Prague

(The following prayers are repeated once a day for nine consecutive days.)

The Sign of the Cross*

Opening Prayers
Eternal Father, I offer to Your honor and glory, for my eternal salvation and that of the whole world, the mystery of the birth of our Divine Redeemer.
Glory Be*

Divine Infant Jesus, bless and protect us.
Eternal Father, I offer to Your honor and glory, for my eternal salvation and that of the whole world, the suffering of the most Holy Virgin and St. Joseph, in the long and weary journey from Nazareth to Bethlehem, and the anguish of their hearts at finding no place of shelter when the Savior of the world was born.
Glory Be

Divine Infant Jesus, bless and protect us.
Eternal Father, I offer to Your honor and glory, for my eternal salvation and that of the whole world, the sufferings of Jesus in the stable where He was born, the cold He suffered, the tears He shed, and His tender cries.
Glory Be

---

*"The Sign of the Cross" and "Glory Be" can be found in "Prayers Common to Novenas," p. 252.

Divine Infant Jesus, bless and protect us.

Eternal Father, I offer to Your honor and glory, for my eternal salvation and that of the whole world, the humility, the mortification, the patience, the charity, and all the virtues of the Child Jesus. I thank You, I love You, and I bless You unceasingly for the ineffable mystery of the Incarnation of the Divine Word.

Glory Be

The Word was made flesh! And dwelt among us.

O God, whose only begotten Son appeared in the substance of our flesh, grant, we beseech You, that through Him whom we acknowledge to be like unto ourselves, we may be inwardly renewed. Amen.

Prayers of Intercession

O Divine Infant Jesus, bestow Your blessing in abundance upon Your Holy Church, upon the Sovereign Pontiff, upon all bishops, priests, deacons, religious, and all the faithful. Grant perseverance to the just, convert sinners, enlighten unbelievers, assist the dying, deliver the souls in purgatory, and extend upon all hearts the sweet empire of Your love. Amen.

O Divine Infant Jesus, bless our nation and make it true to the ideals of freedom, justice, and brotherhood for all. Be close to our president and statesmen; give them vision and courage as they ponder decisions affecting peace and the future of the world. Make me more deeply aware of my heritage, realizing not only my rights but also my duties and responsibilities as a citizen. Make this great land and all its people know clearly Your will, that we may fulfill the destiny ordained for us. Amen.

O Divine Infant Jesus, Prince of Peace, grant us peace throughout the world, that all nations may work together and that there may be an end to war, and that all hearts may acknowledge Your sacred kingship, and that Your kingdom of peace may be established in the whole world. Amen.

O Divine Infant Jesus, watch over us who have come to be with You this day. Remain with us and guide our way in accord with Your will. Shelter us with Your protection both day and night and bring us safely back to our homes and families. Amen.

O Divine Infant Jesus, You came to reveal Your divine love and to restore our dignity as God's children. Inspire the members of Your Church to continue to make You present in the world by service to our brothers and sisters in the vocations of priesthood, religious life, and lay ministry. Amen.

Prayer of Father Cyril to the Infant of Prague

O Child Jesus, I have recourse to You through Your holy Mother. I implore You to assist me in my necessity, for I firmly believe that Your divine power can assist me. I confidently hope to obtain Your holy grace. I love You with my whole heart and my whole soul. I am heartily sorry for all my sins, and I entreat You, O Good Jesus, to give me strength to amend my life. I am firmly resolved never again to offend You, and to suffer anything rather than to displease You. I wish to serve You faithfully. For love of You, O Child Jesus, I will love my neighbor as myself. O Jesus, most powerful Child, I implore You to assist me in this necessity *(mention your request here)*. Grant me the grace of possessing You with Mary and Joseph, and of adoring You with Your holy angels and saints. Amen.

O Divine Infant Jesus, bestow Your most precious graces on our children. Increase in them faith, hope, and love. May Your love lead them to solid piety, inspiring them with dread for sin, love of good, and an ardent desire of worthily approaching Your Holy Table. Preserve in them innocence and purity of heart; and if they should offend You, grant them the grace of a prompt and sincere repentance. From Your throne in heaven watch over them day and night; protect them in all their ways. Grant that they may acquire the knowledge that they need to embrace the state of life to which You have called them. Grant us a sincere love, constant vigilance, and generous devotedness toward them. Grant them all consolation on earth and eternal reward in heaven. Amen.

O Divine Infant Jesus, physician and healer of the sick, we place under Your care those who are sick and suffering. Alleviate their worry, suffering, and pain with Your gentle love. We ask that You heal their sickness and pain and restore them to health, so that they may joyfully witness to the power of Your love. Above all, grant them the grace to acknowledge Your holy will and unite their sufferings and pain with Yours. Amen.

Blessing

May the Infant Jesus be with us that He may defend us; be within us, that He may guide us; follow us, that He may guard us; be with us, that He may bless us; and may the blessing of Almighty God *[make the Sign of the Cross here as you say the following]*, the Father, the Son, and the Holy Spirit descend upon us and remain with us forever. Amen.

Prayer of Thanksgiving

(Said on the final day of the novena.)

I prostrate myself before Your holy Image, O most gracious Infant Jesus, to offer You my most fervent thanks for the blessings You have bestowed on me. I shall incessantly praise Your mercy and confess that You alone are my God, my helper, and my protector. Henceforth my entire confidence shall be placed in You; everywhere will 1 proclaim aloud Your mercy and generosity, so that Your great love and the great deeds which You perform through this miraculous image may be acknowledged by all. May devotion to Your holy infancy extend more and more in the hearts of all Christians, and may all who experience Your assistance persevere with me in showing unceasing gratitude to Your most holy infancy, to which be praise and glory for all eternity. Amen.

National Shrine of the Infant Jesus of Prague

The town of Prague, Oklahoma, was settled by several Bohemian families in 1902 and named after their beloved city in their homeland. In 1909, the bishop of the area dedicated the parish church after St. Wenceslaus, the patron of the Czech republic. This church was destroyed by a tornado ten years later and replaced with a brick structure with the same name.

Soon a larger church was needed and, in 1947, plans were drawn up for a new structure. However, there seemed to be no way the parish could afford to build it. While visiting his ailing mother in California, the pastor mentioned the dire financial situation of his parish. One of the Sisters of Mercy caring for the priest's mother overheard their discussion and suggested entrusting the venture to the Infant of Prague. The nuns presented Father Johnson with a statue of the Infant of Prague in 1947, and when he returned to his parish he placed it in St. Wenceslaus Church. One day while praying in the church, Father Johnson promised the Infant Jesus that he would name the new church in His honor if He would help him get it built.

Not too long thereafter, donations for the new church began pouring in, not only from parishioners in Prague, but miraculously from around the United States. In 1949, the new church was dedicated, with the statue of the Infant of Prague being placed on the main altar.

The National Shrine of the Infant Jesus of Prague
4th and Broadway
Prague, OK 74864
Telephone: 405-567-3080

CHAPTER 2

Sacred Heart of Jesus

Source of Peace and Reconciliation

History of the Devotion

Claude Alacoque and Philiberte Lamyn named the fifth of their seven children Margaret on the day of her birth, July 22, 1647. Margaret, born in Lauthecourt, France, would barely get to know her father before he would die of pneumonia when she was eight. A short time after his death, Margaret was sent away to a convent school where she excelled until, at the age of eleven, she contracted rheumatic fever and then spent the next four years bedridden.

Returning to the family home, Margaret found that her family had fallen on hard times since the death of her father. Claude's relatives now ran the household and treated Philiberte and her children like servants. This sad situation lasted until the eldest of Philiberte's sons finally became of legal age and control of the estate reverted back to Philiberte's family.

Margaret had a deep love for Jesus throughout her childhood. Her strong love for Jesus, present in the Blessed Sacrament, led her, at age twenty-two, to enter the community of nuns founded by St. Francis de Sales called the Order of the Visitation at Paray-le-Monial. This community was founded on principles of humility and selflessness for which Margaret's earlier experiences at the hands of her relatives had prepared her well. Upon her profession, she was given the name Mary, which was added to her given name, Margaret.

On December 27, 1673, the Feast of St. John the Evangelist, Margaret Mary had a unique experience while praying in the presence of the Blessed Sacrament. It seemed to her that she no longer existed as a separate entity. In the midst of this experience, she felt as though Jesus wished for her to take the place of the Beloved Disciple at the Last Supper. She imagined laying her head against the Lord's breast so that she might hear the beat of his heart and know how great was the love that Jesus had for the human race. Jesus shared with Margaret Mary his sadness at how indifferent people were to his love.

Her superior did not take Margaret Mary's prayer experiences seriously. But when Margaret insisted on the validity of them, her superior appointed several theologians to listen to Margaret's story. They concluded that Margaret Mary suffered from delusions. Thus Margaret suffered silently until Father Claude de La Colombière, a Jesuit, was appointed as her spiritual director; only then did she find someone who believed her experiences were indeed genuine.

Margaret Mary continued to experience visions of Jesus. He revealed his heart, pierced after the crucifixion, to Margaret and told her that it symbolized his love. The heart was aflame with love, and the Lord wanted Margaret Mary to make known this love to all the world.

Jesus told her that he wished for a feast celebrating his love on the Friday after the Solemnity of Corpus Christi (the Feast of the Body and Blood or Our Lord; literal translation from Latin: "Body of Christ"). He also made known his wish for a special devotion of the reception of Holy Communion on the first Friday of each month in reparation for the ingratitude of humanity. Margaret Mary relayed all this to her spiritual director, Father de La Colombière, who is largely responsible for the spread of the devotion. Margaret Mary died on October 17, 1690. After a vigorous scrutiny of her life and visions, she was beatified in 1864 and canonized in 1920.

The modern devotion to the Sacred Heart of Jesus spread from Paray-le-Monial in 1907 by Father Mateo Crawley-Boevey, SSCC. The movement urged people to enthrone an image of the Sacred Heart in their homes, to consecrate themselves to the love that Jesus had for them, and to attend Mass and receive Holy Communion for nine consecutive first Fridays as Jesus had instructed St. Margaret Mary. Jesus promised that those who did so would be blessed with the grace of final perseverance and would not die without the opportunity to receive the Last Sacraments of the Church. (The Last Sacraments, or Rites, are actually a number of sacramental rites, including the celebration of the Rite of Reconciliation, Viaticum [Holy Communion "for the journey"], and the Rite of the Anointing of the Sick.)

Novena to the Sacred Heart of Jesus

(The following prayers are repeated once a day for nine consecutive days.)

Opening Prayers

Divine Jesus, You have said, "Ask and you shall receive; seek and you shall find; knock and it shall be opened to you." Behold me kneeling at Your feet, filled with a lively faith and confidence in the promises dictated by Your Sacred Heart to St. Margaret Mary. I come to ask this favor *(mention your request here).*

To whom can I turn if not to You, whose Heart is the Source of all graces and merits? Where should I seek, if not in the treasure that contains all the riches of Your kindness and mercy? Where should I knock, if not at the door through which God gives Himself to us and through which we go to God? I have recourse to You, O Heart of Jesus. In You I find consolation when afflicted, protection when persecuted, strength when burdened with trials, and light in doubt and darkness.

Dear Jesus, I firmly believe that You can grant me the grace I implore, even though it should require a miracle. You have only to will it and my prayer will be granted. I admit that I am most unworthy of Your favors, but this is not a reason for me to be discouraged. You are the God of mercy, and You will not refuse a contrite heart. Cast upon me a look of mercy, I beg of You, and Your kind Heart will find in my miseries and weakness a reason for granting my prayer.

Sacred Heart, whatever may be Your decision with regard to my request, I will never stop adoring, loving, praising, and serving You. My Jesus, be pleased to accept this, my act of perfect resignation to the decrees of Your adorable Heart, which I sincerely desire may be fulfilled in and by me and all Your creatures forever.

Grant me the grace for which I humbly implore You through the Immaculate Heart of Your most sorrowful Mother. You entrusted me to her as her child, and her prayers are all-powerful with You. Amen.

Offering to the Sacred Heart of Jesus

My God, I offer You all my prayers, works, joys, and sufferings in union with the Sacred Heart of Jesus, for the intentions for which He pleads and offers Himself in the Holy Sacrifice of the Mass, in thanksgiving for Your favors, in reparation for my sins, and in humble supplication for my temporal and eternal welfare, for the needs of our holy Mother the Church, for the conversion of sinners, and for the relief of the poor souls in purgatory.

Litany of the Sacred Heart of Jesus

Lord, have mercy. Lord, have mercy.
Christ, have mercy. Christ, have mercy.
Lord, have mercy. Lord, have mercy.
Jesus, hear us. Jesus, graciously hear us.
God, the Father of heaven, have mercy on us.
God, the Son, Redeemer of the world, have mercy on us.
God, the Holy Spirit, have mercy on us.
Holy Trinity, One God, have mercy on us.
Heart of Jesus, Son of the Eternal Father, have mercy on us.

Heart of Jesus, formed in the womb of the Virgin
Mother, have mercy on us.
Heart of Jesus, one with the eternal Word, have mercy
on us.
Heart of Jesus, infinite in majesty, have mercy on us.
Heart of Jesus, holy temple of God, have mercy on us.
Heart of Jesus, tabernacle of the Most High, have
mercy on us.
Heart of Jesus, house of God and gate of heaven, have
mercy on us.
Heart of Jesus, aflame with love for us, have mercy on
us.
Heart of Jesus, source of justice and love, have mercy
on us.
Heart of Jesus, full of goodness and love, have mercy
on us.
Heart of Jesus, wellspring of all virtue, have mercy on
us.
Heart of Jesus, worthy of all praise, have mercy on us.
Heart of Jesus, king and center of all hearts, have
mercy on us.
Heart of Jesus, treasure-house of wisdom and
knowledge, have mercy on us.
Heart of Jesus, in whom dwells the fullness of God,
have mercy on us.
Heart of Jesus, in whom the Father is well-pleased,
have mercy on us.
Heart of Jesus, from whose fullness we have all
received, have mercy on us.
Heart of Jesus, desire of the eternal hills, have mercy
on us.
Heart of Jesus, patient and full of mercy, have mercy
on us.

Heart of Jesus, generous to all who turn to you, have mercy on us.

Heart of Jesus, fountain of life and holiness, have mercy on us.

Heart of Jesus, atonement for our sins, have mercy on us.

Heart of Jesus, overwhelmed with insults, have mercy on us.

Heart of Jesus, broken for our sins, have mercy on us.

Heart of Jesus, obedient even to death, have mercy on us.

Heart of Jesus, pierced by a lance, have mercy on us.

Heart of Jesus, source of all consolation, have mercy on us.

Heart of Jesus, our life and resurrection, have mercy on us.

Heart of Jesus, our peace and reconciliation, have mercy on us.

Heart of Jesus, victim for our sins, have mercy on us.

Heart of Jesus, salvation of those who trust in you, have mercy on us.

Heart of Jesus, hope of those who die in you, have mercy on us.

Heart of Jesus, delight of all the saints, have mercy on us.

Lamb of God, who takes away the sins of the world, have mercy on us.

Lamb of God, who takes away the sins of the world, have mercy on us.

Lamb of God, who takes away the sins of the world, have mercy on us.

Jesus, meek and humble of heart, touch our hearts and make them like your own.

Let us pray:

Father, we rejoice in the gifts of love that we have received from the heart of Jesus, your Son.

Open our hearts to share his life and continue to bless us with his love. We ask this in the name of Jesus the Lord. Amen.

National Shrine of the Sacred Heart of Jesus

Father Girard F. Angelo, the pastor of St. Raphael Church in Harleigh, Pennsylvania, began construction of a shrine dedicated to the Sacred Heart of Jesus in 1974. One year later, the three hundredth anniversary of Jesus' appearance to St. Margaret Mary, the shrine was dedicated on the Feast of the Sacred Heart. Father Angelo never shared the inspiration behind building the shrine, but at the dedication the bishop of Scranton renamed the church saying that it would now be known as the Church of the Sacred Heart.

Since then, pilgrims throughout the United States and Canada have visited the shrine. It is open twenty-four hours a day and there is no fee to enter the shrine grounds. In 1997, the shrine was designated a national shrine.

National Shrine of the Sacred Heart
1 Church Place
Harleigh, PA 18225
Telephone: 570-455-1162

CHAPTER 3
Divine Mercy

"Have mercy on us and on the whole world!"

Origin of the Devotion

Helena Kowalska was born on August 25, 1905, in Glogowiec, Poland, to Stanislaus and Marianna. Her parents were poor farmers who were strong in their Catholic faith.

Helena early on exhibited a deep sense of the presence of Jesus in the Blessed Sacrament. One day, the seven-year-old Helena was with her family for Exposition of the Blessed Sacrament at her local church. While the family prayed, Helena experienced Jesus speaking to her personally. He invited her to live a more perfect life.

Helena also experienced an overpowering light that sometimes would keep her from sleeping at night. Her parents tried to squelch what they perceived as her overactive imagination, but their attempts to convince her otherwise did not make the lights go away. Once, while working as a maid, Helena experienced her "lights" during the day. It seemed to her that the entire courtyard was on fire, and she yelled for help. When the woman of the house came running, ready to put out the fire, there was no fire visible to her.

When she turned seventeen, Helena asked her parents for permission to enter the convent. They were against it, mostly out of concern for the financial burden of paying the dowry that a convent would have required at that time. At first she was obedient to her parents' wishes, but Jesus continued to speak to her, urging her to go to Warsaw where she would find acceptance in a religious community. Finally, at the age of twenty, she set out for Warsaw.

When she arrived in Warsaw, she found that the religious communities were unwilling to accept her, mainly due to the fact that she offered no dowry or special skill that the nuns could use. Finally the Sisters of Our Lady of Mercy agreed to accept her if she would work to pay for the cost of her clothing needed for religious life, her habit. Once she had done this, she entered the community and was given the name Mary Faustina.

Sister Faustina soon found that religious life was not what she had expected. Her days were filled with washing floors and clothes and working in the kitchen (not unlike the tasks she had done working as a maid). After only a few weeks, she began to wonder if she might not belong in a place where they prayed more. In the midst of such thoughts Jesus appeared to Faustina, his face badly bruised and cut. When Faustina asked the Lord who had hurt him so much, he replied that she had, by her doubts that this convent wasn't where he wished her to be.

When Sister Faustina made her vows to the Lord and the community, she was made aware of how much she would suffer. She suffered physically from consumption, or tuberculosis, and asthma. She also suffered mentally from her own doubts and from being misunderstood by others in her community. She accepted all these afflictions as a way of participating in the suffering of Jesus.

In 1931, when Sister Faustina was twenty-six, Jesus told her he wished to have an image painted of himself that would convey his great mercy for humankind. Not being gifted as an artist herself, Sister Faustina found this a difficult request to fulfill. In 1934, she finally found an artist who would paint the picture that now is well known as the Divine Mercy image.

Faithful to the request of her spiritual director, she recorded all that occurred during her mystical experiences. Her diary details that Jesus wanted her to announce the great love God has for all of his creation. Through Faustina, Jesus spoke of his desire that all would trust in the great mercy of God and abandon themselves to God's love. The mercy of God, according to Faustina's writings, is so great that every sin can be forgiven if sinners would only turn to Jesus and abandon themselves to that mercy.

Faustina died at the age of thirty-three on October 5, 1938. The novena in honor of Divine Mercy is taken from the diary of Sister Faustina and originally was prayed by her. Jesus asked that a different group of souls in need of mercy be especially prayed for every day. When one contrasts the shortness and relative obscurity of Sister Faustina's life with the popularity of this devotion today, one is left in awe of the power of God to use the smallest things to accomplish his designs. Sister Mary Faustina was declared Blessed by Pope John Paul II, an ardent supporter of Sister Faustina, on April 18, 1993.

Novena in Honor
of the Divine Mercy

The Novena of Divine Mercy begins with the recitation of the Chaplet of Divine Mercy followed by the prayer for the specific day of the novena.

How to Recite the Chaplet of Divine Mercy
(The Chaplet of Divine Mercy is recited using ordinary rosary beads of five decades.)

1. Begin the chaplet with one Our Father, one Hail Mary, and the Apostles' Creed.*

2. Then, on the large bead before each decade, say: "Eternal Father, I offer You the Body and Blood, Soul and Divinity, of Your dearly beloved Son, Our Lord Jesus Christ, in atonement for our sins and those of the whole world."

3. Next, on the ten small beads of each decade, say: "For the sake of His sorrowful Passion, have mercy on us and on the whole world."

4. Conclude with: "Holy God, Holy Mighty One, Holy Immortal One, have mercy on us and on the whole world *[three times]*."

---

*The "Our Father," "Hail Mary," and "Apostles' Creed" can all be found in "Prayers Common to Novenas," p. 252.

FIRST DAY

Today bring to me all mankind, especially all sinners.

(Pray the Chaplet of Divine Mercy on p. 49.)

Novena Prayer

Most Merciful Jesus, whose very nature it is to have compassion on us and to forgive us, do not look upon our sins but upon our trust which we place in Your infinite goodness. Receive us all into the abode of Your Most Compassionate Heart, and never let us escape from it. We beg this of You by Your love which unites You to the Father and the Holy Spirit.

Eternal Father, turn Your merciful gaze upon all mankind and especially upon poor sinners, all enfolded in the Most Compassionate Heart of Jesus. For the sake of His sorrowful Passion show us Your mercy, that we may praise the omnipotence of Your mercy for ever and ever. Amen.

SECOND DAY

Today bring to me the souls of priests and religious.

(Pray the Chaplet of Divine Mercy on p. 49.)

Novena Prayer

Most Merciful Jesus, from whom comes all that is good, increase Your grace in men and women consecrated to Your service, that they may perform worthy works of mercy; and that all who see them may glorify the Father of Mercy who is in heaven.

Eternal Father, turn Your merciful gaze upon the company of chosen ones in Your vineyard — upon the souls of priests and religious; and endow them with the strength of Your blessing. For the love of the Heart of Your Son in which they are enfolded, impart to them Your power and light, that they may be able to guide others in the way of salvation and with one voice sing praise to Your boundless mercy for ages without end. Amen.

THIRD DAY

Today bring to me all devout and faithful souls.

(Pray the Chaplet of Divine Mercy on p. 49.)

Novena Prayer

Most Merciful Jesus, from the treasury of Your mercy You impart Your graces in great abundance to each and all. Receive us into the abode of Your Most Compassionate Heart and never let us escape from it. We beg this grace of You by that most wondrous love for the heavenly Father with which Your Heart burns so fiercely.

Eternal Father, turn Your merciful gaze upon faithful souls, as upon the inheritance of Your Son. For the sake of His sorrowful Passion, grant them Your blessing and surround them with Your constant protection. Thus may they never fail in love or lose the treasure of the holy faith, but rather, with all the hosts of Angels and Saints, may they glorify Your boundless mercy for endless ages. Amen.

FOURTH DAY

Today bring to me those who do not believe in God and those who do not yet know me.

(Pray the Chaplet of Divine Mercy on p. 49.)

Novena Prayer

Most compassionate Jesus, You are the Light of the whole world. Receive into the abode of Your Most Compassionate Heart the souls of those who do not believe in God and of those who as yet do not know You. Let the rays of Your grace enlighten them that they, too, together with us, may extol Your wonderful mercy; and do not let them escape from the abode which is Your Most Compassionate Heart.

Eternal Father, turn Your merciful gaze upon the souls of those who do not believe in You, and of those who as yet do not know You but who are enclosed in the Most Compassionate Heart of Jesus. Draw them to the light of the Gospel. These souls do not know what great happiness it is to love You. Grant that they, too, may extol the generosity of Your mercy for endless ages. Amen.

FIFTH DAY

Today bring to me the souls of those who have separated themselves from my Church.

(Pray the Chaplet of Divine Mercy on p. 49.)

Novena Prayer

Most Merciful Jesus, Goodness Itself, You do not refuse light to those who seek it of You. Receive into the abode of Your Most Compassionate Heart the souls of those who have separated themselves from Your Church. Draw them by Your light into the unity of the Church and do not let them escape from the abode of Your Most Compassionate Heart; but bring it about that they, too, may come to glorify the generosity of Your mercy.

Eternal Father, turn Your merciful gaze upon the souls of those who have separated themselves from Your Son's Church, who have squandered Your blessings and misused Your graces by obstinately persisting in their errors. Do not look upon their errors, but upon the love of Your own Son and upon His bitter Passion, which He underwent for their sake, since they, too, are enclosed in His Most Compassionate Heart. Bring it about that they also may glorify Your great mercy for endless ages. Amen.

SIXTH DAY

Today bring to me the meek and humble souls and the souls of little children.

(Pray the Chaplet of Divine Mercy on p. 49.)

Novena Prayer

Most Merciful Jesus, You Yourself have said, "Learn from me for I am meek and humble of heart." Receive into the abode of Your Most Compassionate Heart all meek and humble souls and the souls of little children. These souls send all heaven into ecstasy and they are the heavenly Father's favorites. They are a sweet-smelling bouquet before the throne of God; God Himself takes delight in their fragrance. These souls have a permanent abode in Your Most Compassionate Heart, O Jesus, and they unceasingly sing out a hymn of love and mercy.

Eternal Father, turn Your merciful gaze upon meek souls, upon humble souls, and upon little children who are enfolded in the abode which is the Most Compassionate Heart of Jesus. These souls bear the closest resemblance to Your Son. Their fragrance rises from the earth and reaches Your very throne. Father of mercy and of all goodness, I beg You by the love You bear these souls and by the delight You take in them: Bless the whole world, that all souls together may sing out the praises of Your mercy for endless ages. Amen.

SEVENTH DAY

Today bring to me the souls who especially venerate and glorify my mercy.

(Pray the Chaplet of Divine Mercy on p. 49.)

Novena Prayer

Most Merciful Jesus, whose Heart is Love Itself, receive into the abode of Your Most Compassionate Heart the souls of those who particularly extol and venerate the greatness of Your mercy. These souls are mighty with the very power of God Himself. In the midst of all afflictions and adversities they go forward, confident of Your mercy; and united to You, O Jesus, they carry all mankind on their shoulders. These souls will not be judged severely, but Your mercy will embrace them as they depart from this life.

Eternal Father, turn Your merciful gaze upon the souls who glorify and venerate Your greatest attribute, that of Your fathomless mercy, and who are enclosed in the Most Compassionate Heart of Jesus. These souls are a living Gospel; their hands are full of deeds of mercy, and their hearts, overflowing with joy, sing a canticle of mercy to You, O Most High! I beg You, O God: Show them Your mercy according to the hope and trust they have placed in You. Let there be accomplished in them the promise of Jesus, who said to them that during their life, but especially at the hour of death, the souls who will venerate this fathomless mercy of His, He Himself will defend as His glory. Amen.

EIGHTH DAY

Today bring to me the souls who are detained in purgatory.

(Pray the Chaplet of Divine Mercy on p. 49.)

Novena Prayer

Most Merciful Jesus, You Yourself have said that You desire mercy; so I bring into the abode of Your Most Compassionate Heart the souls in purgatory, souls who are very dear to You, and yet, who must make retribution to Your justice. May the streams of Blood and Water which gushed forth from Your Heart put out the flames of purgatory, that there, too, the power of Your mercy may be celebrated.

Eternal Father, turn Your merciful gaze upon the souls suffering in purgatory, who are enfolded in the Most Compassionate Heart of Jesus. I beg You, by the sorrowful Passion of Jesus Your Son, and by all the bitterness with which His most sacred Soul was flooded: Manifest Your mercy to the souls who are under Your just scrutiny. Look upon them in no other way but only through the Wounds of Jesus, Your dearly beloved Son; for we firmly believe that there is no limit to Your goodness and compassion. Amen.

NINTH DAY

Today bring to me souls who have become lukewarm.

(Pray the Chaplet of Divine Mercy on p. 49.)

Novena Prayer

Most compassionate Jesus, You are Compassion Itself. I bring lukewarm souls into the abode of Your Most Compassionate Heart. In this fire of Your pure love let these tepid souls, who, like corpses, filled You with such deep loathing, be once again set aflame. O Most Compassionate Jesus, exercise the omnipotence of Your mercy and draw them into the very ardor of Your love, and bestow upon them the gift of holy love, for nothing is beyond Your power.

Eternal Father, turn Your merciful gaze upon lukewarm souls who are nonetheless enfolded in the Most Compassionate Heart of Jesus. Father of Mercy, I beg You by the bitter Passion of Your Son and by His three-hour agony on the Cross: Let them, too, glorify the abyss of Your mercy. Amen.

National Shrine of the Divine Mercy

The National Shrine of the Divine Mercy was built in the 1950s on Eden Hill in Stockbridge, Massachusetts. The shrine is home to a copy of the sacred image of Jesus envisioned by Blessed Faustina in 1931. In the sanctuary of the shrine there is a wood carving of Blessed Faustina and a first-class relic (a bone from her foot). There is also a wood carving of Blessed George Matulaitis-Matulewicz (renovator of the Marians of the Immaculate Conception) and a second-class relic of his.

Daily at three o'clock, the hour Jesus died on the cross, the shrine bells ring and announce to all the great mercy of the Son of God, who gave his life as ransom for the many. The Chaplet of Divine Mercy is prayed at this time each day at the shrine.

National Shrine of the Divine Mercy
P.O. Box 951, Eden Hill
Stockbridge, MA 01262
Telephone: 413-298-3931
E-mail: sr.bettwy@marian.org
Website: http://www.marian.org/

Part 2

Novena to the Holy Spirit

"Do not leave Jerusalem, but wait for the gift my Father promised, which you have heard me speak about. For John baptized with water, but in a few days you will be baptized with the Holy Spirit."

ACTS 1:4-5

CHAPTER 4
St. Maximilian Kolbe

Apostle of Charity

Life of St. Maximilian Kolbe

Raymond Kolbe was born in Poland on January 8, 1894, to Maria Dabrowka and Julius Kolbe. While Raymond was still very young, Maria instilled within him a deep love of the Blessed Virgin Mary and devotion to her by teaching him to pray the Rosary and the *Angelus*.

One day, when Raymond was acting less than saintly, Maria scolded him, wondering aloud what would ever become of him. A dejected young Raymond went to kneel before a statue of the Blessed Virgin Mary to ask her opinion on the matter. In response, Mary appeared before him holding a red crown and a white crown. Looking down at Raymond, she asked him which he preferred. He chose both. The apparition symbolized the life he was to lead: chastity symbolized by the white crown and martyrdom symbolized by the red one.

At age thirteen, Raymond entered the Franciscan minor seminary at Lwow, along with his brother Francis. His time there was one of occasional struggle over the uncertainty of his vocation. Was he to be a soldier for Mary in the military or the priesthood? A surprise visit from his mother led him to understand God's will in the matter: he was to be a Franciscan priest. On November 1, 1914, he took perpetual vows as a Franciscan, taking the name Maximilian. The next few years of his life were spent studying in Rome, where he earned doctorates in philosophy and theology despite suffering from tuberculosis. He was ordained a priest on April 28, 1918.

The previous year, on October 16, 1917, Maximilian and six other friars formed the Militia of the Immaculata (MI) — a group he envisioned would use every modern technique available to spread the Gospel message and total consecration to Mary. The motivation to form the MI arose from an incident involving antipapal demonstrations of Freemasons in St. Peter's Square in Rome.

After his ordination, he returned to Poland and began the work of spreading the MI by establishing a magazine called the *Knight of the Immaculata*. By 1927, he was forced to find larger facilities for his expanding printing apostolate and established Niepokalanow (or "City of the Immaculata") near Warsaw.

In his magazine and other publications, Maximilian wrote extensively about the role of Mary in God's plan of salvation. He saw Mary's statement to St. Bernadette at Lourdes, "I am the Immaculate Conception," as a testimony of the intimacy that Mary shared with the Holy Trinity. She alone from the first moment of her conception enjoyed a permanent and "inexpressible union" with the Holy Spirit like no other human being before or since. Kolbe saw Mary as prepared by the Father from all eternity to be the tabernacle of the Living God. She was the perfect complement to the Holy Trinity.

In 1930, Maximilian and four other friars from Niepokalanow traveled to Nagasaki, Japan, to establish a new "City of the Immaculata." He taught for a while in the diocesan seminary, and it was shortly after this time that he began publishing *Seibo no Kishi* (Japanese for "Knight of the Immaculata"), a magazine designed to foster devotion to Jesus and Mary. Soon afterward, in 1931, he opened a friary in Nagasaki. He was recalled to Poland in 1936 and resumed direction of Niepokalanow once again as its guardian.

When World War II began in 1939, Maximilian and thirty-five other friars were arrested and held for three months by the Nazis. After being released, he obtained permission to print one issue of his magazine. Shortly afterward, he was arrested once again, in February 1941, since he was viewed as dangerous by the Nazis. This time he was tortured by them and eventually sent to the concentration camp in Auschwitz.

At Auschwitz, after a prisoner had escaped, the commandant of the death camp selected ten men from a lineup of the prisoners to undergo death by starvation, including a family man, Francis Gajowniczek. Father Maximilian was not one of those chosen but stepped forward offering to take Gajowniczek's place. The commandant accepted the priest's offer. Placed in a small bunker and deprived of all food, half of the condemned men died in less than two weeks, but Father Kolbe and four others survived for two weeks. On August 14, 1941, needing the bunker for other prisoners, the commandant ordered the remaining men to be killed. Father Maximilian was injected lethally with carbolic acid. The following day, the Feast of Mary's Assumption, he was cremated in one of the camp's furnaces.

Pope John Paul II canonized Maximilian Kolbe on October 10, 1982, and declared him to be a "martyr of charity" and, later, "patron of our difficult century." Francis Gajowniczek, who was at the canonization, witnessed the declaration of sainthood of the man who had taken his place in the starvation bunker some forty-one years before.

The Holy Father had recently developed our understanding of Kolbe's significance even further. He has called him an "apostle of a 'new Marian era,' " because of his profound, groundbreaking Marian theology, and a "prophet of the civilization of love," because of his martyrdom of love for another amidst our encroaching culture of death.

St. Maximilian Kolbe is considered the patron of journalists, prisoners, families, the pro-life movement, and, because of his manner of death, those with eating disorders and chemical addictions.

Novena to the Holy Spirit

Under the Direction of Faith

Prayer of St. Maximilian Kolbe

O my God, my only happiness — how can I come to know you more perfectly? I see your creatures and I am enchanted; I give thanks and I love you, but these do not suffice for me, as you know so well; but I do not see or hear you. I desire to become like unto you according to your will, but how? You are most pure Spirit, and I am flesh. Make known to me how I, man of flesh, must perfect myself and become like you, most Holy Spirit, to be raised to the divine life.

Reading

The Holy Spirit says in Sacred Scripture: "The just man lives by faith." He does not say that he lives by reason or intelligence, but by faith, for human reason and intelligence are limited in concept and in conceptualization, and, consequently, do not fathom many things in the realm of nature, not to mention in the realm of the supernatural life and the mysteries of God. Here, only faith comes to our assistance. As a divine virtue it enlightens and illuminates — and illustrates — the truths of God that are not accessible to reason. A man who is guided only by reason will frequently err and fall by the wayside.

(From an article by St. Maximilian Kolbe, January 17, 1937.)

Reflection

Do I seek the Spirit's enlightenment to deepen my understanding of the faith?

Novena Prayer

Father of light and of love, from whom every good gift comes, send forth the power of your Spirit into our lives to renew the Church in this new millennium. Open our minds and hearts, and fill us with the virtues of faith, hope, and charity. Loosen our tongues to sing your praises and to proclaim the Gospel of Salvation to all. Use us as bold instruments of the New Evangelization, in union with the Immaculate Virgin Mary and St. Maximilian Kolbe. Help us to realize that without your Spirit we could never bring peace and reconciliation to our broken world nor announce the truth that Jesus Christ is Lord. We ask all these things *(mention your request here)* in Jesus' name, who lives and reigns with you and the Holy Spirit, one God, forever and ever. Amen.

SECOND DAY
Who Is the Holy Spirit?

Prayer of St. Maximilian Kolbe

O my God, my only happiness — how can I come to know you more perfectly? I see your creatures and I am enchanted; I give thanks and I love you, but these do not suffice for me, as you know so well; but I do not see or hear you. I desire to become like unto you according to your will, but how? You are most pure Spirit, and I am flesh. Make known to me how I, man of flesh, must perfect myself and become like you, most Holy Spirit, to be raised to the divine life.

Reading

And who is the Holy Spirit? The flowering of the love of the Father and the Son. If the fruit of created love is a created conception, then the fruit of Divine Love, that prototype of all created love, is necessarily a divine "conception." The Holy Spirit is, therefore, the "uncreated eternal conception," the prototype of all the conceptions that multiply life throughout the whole universe.

(From St. Maximilian's last writing, his spiritual testament, February 17, 1941.)

Reflection

Does my love for God blossom into the lives of others?

Novena Prayer

Father of light and of love, from whom every good gift comes, send forth the power of your Spirit into our lives to renew the Church in this new millennium. Open our minds and hearts, and fill us with the virtues of faith, hope, and charity. Loosen our tongues to sing your praises and to proclaim the Gospel of Salvation to all. Use us as bold instruments of the New Evangelization, in union with the Immaculate Virgin Mary and St. Maximilian Kolbe. Help us to realize that without your Spirit, we could never bring peace and reconciliation to our broken world nor announce the truth that Jesus Christ is Lord. We ask all these things *(mention your request here)* in Jesus' name, who lives and reigns with you and the Holy Spirit, one God, forever and ever. Amen.

THIRD DAY

The Spirit — The "Conception" of Love

Prayer of St. Maximilian Kolbe

O my God, my only happiness — how can I come to know you more perfectly? I see your creatures and I am enchanted; I give thanks and I love you, but these do not suffice for me, as you know so well; but I do not see or hear you. I desire to become like unto you according to your will, but how? You are most pure Spirit, and I am flesh. Make known to me how I, man of flesh, must perfect myself and become like you, most Holy Spirit, to be raised to the divine life.

Reading

The Father begets; the Son is begotten; the Spirit is the "conception" that springs from their love; there we have the intimate life of the three Persons by which they can be distinguished one from another. But they are united in the oneness of their nature, of their divine existence. The Spirit is, then, this thrice-holy "conception," this infinitely holy "immaculate conception."

(From St. Maximilian's last writing, his spiritual testament, February 17, 1941.)

Reflection

Do I pray regularly to deepen my intimacy with God?

Novena Prayer

Father of light and of love, from whom every good gift comes, send forth the power of your Spirit into our lives to renew the Church in this new millennium. Open our minds and hearts, and fill us with the virtues of faith, hope, and charity. Loosen our tongues to sing your praises and to proclaim the Gospel of Salvation to all. Use us as bold instruments of the New Evangelization, in union with the Immaculate Virgin Mary and St. Maximilian Kolbe. Help us to realize that without your Spirit, we could never bring peace and reconciliation to our broken world nor announce the truth that Jesus Christ is Lord. We ask all these things *(mention your request here)* in Jesus' name, who lives and reigns with you and the Holy Spirit, one God, forever and ever. Amen.

FOURTH DAY

The Relationship Between the Holy Spirit
and the Blessed Virgin

Prayer of St. Maximilian Kolbe

O my God, my only happiness — how can I come to know you more perfectly? I see your creatures and I am enchanted; I give thanks and I love you, but these do not suffice for me, as you know so well; but I do not see or hear you. I desire to become like unto you according to your will, but how? You are most pure Spirit, and I am flesh. Make known to me how I, man of flesh, must perfect myself and become like you, most Holy Spirit, to be raised to the divine life.

Reading

In the union of the Holy Spirit with her [the Blessed Virgin], not only do we have the love of two beings; in one of the two we have all the love of the Trinity itself; and in the other we have all of creation's love. Hence, in this union heaven and earth meet; all of heaven with all of earth, the totality of divine eternal love with the plenitude of created love. It is the true summit of love. . . .

The Holy Spirit dwells in the Immaculata, lives in her, and does so from the first instant of her existence, and thenceforth forever.

(From St. Maximilian's last writing, his spiritual testament, February 17, 1941.)

Reflection

Do I renew my total consecration to Mary daily so as to draw closer to the Spirit?

Novena Prayer

Father of light and of love, from whom every good gift comes, send forth the power of your Spirit into our lives to renew the Church in this new millennium. Open our minds and hearts, and fill us with the virtues of faith, hope, and charity. Loosen our tongues to sing your praises and to proclaim the Gospel of Salvation to all. Use us as bold instruments of the New Evangelization, in union with the Immaculate Virgin Mary and St. Maximilian Kolbe. Help us to realize that without your Spirit, we could never bring peace and reconciliation to our broken world nor announce the truth that Jesus Christ is Lord. We ask all these things *(mention your request here)* in Jesus' name, who lives and reigns with you and the Holy Spirit, one God, forever and ever. Amen.

FIFTH DAY

The Blessed Virgin in Whom We Venerate the Holy Spirit

Prayer of St. Maximilian Kolbe

O my God, my only happiness — how can I come to
know you more perfectly? I see your creatures and I am
enchanted; I give thanks and I love you, but these do not
suffice for me, as you know so well; but I do not see or hear
you. I desire to become like unto you according to your will,
but how? You are most pure Spirit, and I am flesh. Make
known to me how I, man of flesh, must perfect myself and
become like you, most Holy Spirit, to be raised to the divine
life.

Reading

Our heavenly Father is the source of all that is;
everything comes from the Blessed Trinity. We cannot see
God, and so Jesus came to this earth, to make him known to
us. The Most Blessed Virgin is the one in whom we venerate
the Holy Spirit, for she is his spouse. . . .

The third Person of the Blessed Trinity never took
flesh; still, our human word "spouse" is far too weak to
express the reality of the relationship between the
Immaculata and the Holy Spirit. We can affirm that she is, in
a certain sense, the "incarnation" of the Holy Spirit. It is the
Holy Spirit that we love in her; and through her we love the
Son. The Holy Spirit is far too little known. . . .

(From a conference by St. Maximilian, February 5, 1941.)

Reflection

Do I invoke the Spirit's inspiration and guidance
throughout the day?

Novena Prayer

Father of light and of love, from whom every good gift comes, send forth the power of your Spirit into our lives to renew the Church in this new millennium. Open our minds and hearts, and fill us with the virtues of faith, hope, and charity. Loosen our tongues to sing your praises and to proclaim the Gospel of Salvation to all. Use us as bold instruments of the New Evangelization, in union with the Immaculate Virgin Mary and St. Maximilian Kolbe. Help us to realize that without your Spirit, we could never bring peace and reconciliation to our broken world nor announce the truth that Jesus Christ is Lord. We ask all these things *(mention your request here)* in Jesus' name, who lives and reigns with you and the Holy Spirit, one God, forever and ever. Amen.

SIXTH DAY
The Indwelling of the Holy Spirit

Prayer of St. Maximilian Kolbe

O my God, my only happiness — how can I come to know you more perfectly? I see your creatures and I am enchanted; I give thanks and I love you, but these do not suffice for me, as you know so well; but I do not see or hear you. I desire to become like unto you according to your will, but how? You are most pure Spirit, and I am flesh. Make known to me how I, man of flesh, must perfect myself and become like you, most Holy Spirit, to be raised to the divine life.

Reading

It is said that the Holy Spirit dwells in the souls of the just. If this is so, then he must dwell in the most perfect manner possible in the soul of the Immaculata. Our Most Holy Mother is totally diffused with the divine. For this reason we call her the spouse of the Holy Spirit, even though we know that this name is only a distant shadow of the reality. For the Holy Spirit fashioned the humanity of Jesus in her womb, in a miraculous manner. If Jesus says of the souls of the just: "We will make our abode in them" (John 14:23), then what an immense difference there must be between us and our most Blessed Mother, in regard to this indwelling!

(From a conference by St. Maximilian, April 9, 1938.)

Reflection

Do I examine my conscience regularly so as to make myself a more fitting place for the Spirit's indwelling?

Novena Prayer

Father of light and of love, from whom every good gift comes, send forth the power of your Spirit into our lives to renew the Church in this new millennium. Open our minds and hearts, and fill us with the virtues of faith, hope, and charity. Loosen our tongues to sing your praises and to proclaim the Gospel of Salvation to all. Use us as bold instruments of the New Evangelization, in union with the Immaculate Virgin Mary and St. Maximilian Kolbe. Help us to realize that without your Spirit, we could never bring peace and reconciliation to our broken world nor announce the truth that Jesus Christ is Lord. We ask all these things *(mention your request here)* in Jesus' name, who lives and reigns with you and the Holy Spirit, one God, forever and ever. Amen.

SEVENTH DAY
The Holy Spirit Makes the Blessed Virgin Fruitful

Prayer of St. Maximilian Kolbe

O my God, my only happiness — how can I come to know you more perfectly? I see your creatures and I am enchanted; I give thanks and I love you, but these do not suffice for me, as you know so well; but I do not see or hear you. I desire to become like unto you according to your will, but how? You are most pure Spirit, and I am flesh. Make known to me how I, man of flesh, must perfect myself and become like you, most Holy Spirit, to be raised to the divine life.

Reading

Among creatures made in God's image, the union brought about by married love is the most intimate of all. In a much more precise, more interior, more essential manner, the Holy Spirit lives in the soul of the Immaculata, in the depths of her very being. He makes her fruitful from the very first instant of her existence, all during her life, and for all eternity. This eternal "Immaculate Conception" (which is the Holy Spirit) produces, in an immaculate manner, divine life itself in the womb (or depths) of Mary's soul, making her the Immaculate Conception, the human Immaculate Conception. The virginal womb of Mary's body is kept sacred for him; there he conceives in time — because everything that is material happens in time — the human life of the man-God.

(From St. Maximilian's last writing, his spiritual testament, February 17, 1941.)

Reflection

How often do I go to confession in order to make my personal apostolate or ministry fruitful?

Novena Prayer

Father of light and of love, from whom every good gift comes, send forth the power of your Spirit into our lives to renew the Church in this new millennium. Open our minds and hearts, and fill us with the virtues of faith, hope, and charity. Loosen our tongues to sing your praises and to proclaim the Gospel of Salvation to all. Use us as bold instruments of the New Evangelization, in union with the Immaculate Virgin Mary and St. Maximilian Kolbe. Help us to realize that without your Spirit, we could never bring peace and reconciliation to our broken world nor announce the truth that Jesus Christ is Lord. We ask all these things *(mention your request here)* in Jesus' name, who lives and reigns with you and the Holy Spirit, one God, forever and ever. Amen.

EIGHTH DAY

How the Holy Spirit Confers Graces

Prayer of St. Maximilian Kolbe

O my God, my only happiness — how can I come to know you more perfectly? I see your creatures and I am enchanted; I give thanks and I love you, but these do not suffice for me, as you know so well; but I do not see or hear you. I desire to become like unto you according to your will, but how? You are most pure Spirit, and I am flesh. Make known to me how I, man of flesh, must perfect myself and become like you, most Holy Spirit, to be raised to the divine life.

Reading

Every grace comes from the Father in consideration of the Son whom he begets from all eternity. And the Holy Spirit who proceeds from the Father and from the Son uses these graces to shape souls to resemblance with the Firstborn, the God-man; he does this in the Immaculata and by her.

(From a conference by St. Maximilian, undated.)

The union between the Immaculata and the Holy Spirit is so inexpressible, yet so perfect, that the Holy Spirit acts only by the Most Blessed Virgin, his Spouse. This is why she is the Mediatrix of all graces given by the Holy Spirit; it follows that there is no grace which Mary cannot dispose of as her own, which is not given to her for this purpose.

(From a letter by St. Maximilian to Father Mikolajczyk, July 28, 1935.)

Reflection

Do I seek Mary's maternal mediation to seek the graces I need to help bring about the kingdom of God?

Novena Prayer

Father of light and of love, from whom every good gift comes, send forth the power of your Spirit into our lives to renew the Church in this new millennium. Open our minds and hearts, and fill us with the virtues of faith, hope, and charity. Loosen our tongues to sing your praises and to proclaim the Gospel of Salvation to all. Use us as bold instruments of the New Evangelization, in union with the Immaculate Virgin Mary and St. Maximilian Kolbe. Help us to realize that without your Spirit, we could never bring peace and reconciliation to our broken world nor announce the truth that Jesus Christ is Lord. We ask all these things *(mention your request here)* in Jesus' name, who lives and reigns with you and the Holy Spirit, one God, forever and ever. Amen.

NINTH DAY
The Holy Spirit Sanctifies Us

Prayer of St. Maximilian Kolbe

O my God, my only happiness — how can I come to know you more perfectly? I see your creatures and I am enchanted; I give thanks and I love you, but these do not suffice for me, as you know so well; but I do not see or hear you. I desire to become like unto you according to your will, but how? You are most pure Spirit, and I am flesh. Make known to me how I, man of flesh, must perfect myself and become like you, most Holy Spirit, to be raised to the divine life.

Reading

The Third Person of the Holy Trinity has a part in this work: he it is who transforms men's souls into temples, souls won by the redemption of Christ, adopted children of God; he makes us heirs of the heavenly kingdom, as St. Paul says: "You are washed and justified in the name of our Lord Jesus

Christ and in the Spirit of our God." It pertains to the Holy Spirit until the end of the world to form the new members of the Mystical Body of Christ's predestined.

(From "The Immaculate Conception of the Blessed Virgin Mary and the Mediation of All Graces," in Miles Immaculatae, *a Latin quarterly for priests by Maximilian Kolbe, 1938.)*

Reflection

Do I seek the Spirit's many gifts to be a more effective evangelist in order to bring about the conversion and sanctification of others?

Novena Prayer

Father of light and of love, from whom every good gift comes, send forth the power of your Spirit into our lives to renew the Church in this new millennium. Open our minds and hearts, and fill us with the virtues of faith, hope, and charity. Loosen our tongues to sing your praises and to proclaim the Gospel of Salvation to all. Use us as bold instruments of the New Evangelization, in union with the Immaculate Virgin Mary and St. Maximilian Kolbe. Help us to realize that without your Spirit, we could never bring peace and reconciliation to our broken world nor announce the truth that Jesus Christ is Lord. We ask all these things *(mention your request here)* in Jesus' name, who lives and reigns with you and the Holy Spirit, one God, forever and ever. Amen.

St. Maximilian Kolbe Shrine

The St. Maximilian Kolbe Shrine in Marytown continues to do the work of its founder, St. Maximilian, by encouraging people to consecrate themselves to Mary Immaculate. The church is a replica of St. Paul's Outside the Walls in Rome, Italy. The Blessed Sacrament is exposed for perpetual adoration and the church is always open.

The life of St. Maximilian Kolbe is depicted on eleven-foot-tall mosaics that decorate the shrine interior. A reliquary within the shrine contains a first-class relic of the saint, some hair from the saint's head saved by a pious barber who had an intuition that Kolbe would one day be canonized. Also in the chapel are a prayer book and pieces of one of the Franciscan habits worn by St. Maximilian.

In the Kolbe Holocaust display is a pictorial memorial that relates the suffering of all who were interned in concentration camps during the Nazi occupation of Poland and, in particular, St. Maximilian Kolbe's experience at Auschwitz. Included in the display is a model of the cement bunker where the martyr and his fellow captives remained imprisoned and subjected to starvation before being injected with the lethal acid that killed them.

Marytown/St. Maximilian Kolbe
1600 West Park Avenue
Libertyville, IL 60048-2593
Telephone: 847-367-7800
Website: http://www.marytown.org/shrine.html

Part 3

Novenas to the Blessed Virgin Mary

"Do whatever he tells you."
JOHN 2:5

"Mary is the perfect *Orans* (pray-er), a figure of the Church. When we pray to her, we are adhering with her to the plan of the Father, who sends his Son to save all men. Like the beloved disciple we welcome Jesus' mother into our homes, for she has become the mother of all the living. We can pray with and to her. The prayer of the Church is sustained by the prayer of Mary and united with it in hope."

CATECHISM OF THE CATHOLIC CHURCH, NO. 2679

CHAPTER 5

The Immaculate Conception

Patroness of the United States of America

History of the Devotion

In August of 1492, Christopher Columbus, accompanied by two other ships, set out on a journey aboard a ship named the *Santa María* (Spanish for "St. Mary," or "Holy Mary") that would take him and his co-adventurers to the New World. Whatever might be said about Columbus today, he certainly was a devotee of the Blessed Virgin. At the close of each day he would gather his crew on the deck where they would chant the *Salve Regina* (Latin for "Hail, Holy Queen"). When the expedition finally made landfall, Columbus named the first place he stopped San Salvador (Spanish for "Holy Savior"), in honor of Jesus. The second place he named Santa María de la Concepción (literally, "Holy Mary of the Conception"), after his love of the teaching that Mary had been conceived without original sin. Thus begins the connection the New World would have to the doctrine of Mary's Immaculate Conception.

Father Andrew White, an early Jesuit missionary, followed Columbus's lead when, in 1640, he declared the Americas to be under the patronage of the Holy Redeemer and the Immaculate Virgin. In 1846, the bishops of the United States petitioned the Holy Father to grant that their country would enjoy the protection of the Blessed Virgin Mary under the title of the Immaculate Conception. The pope granted the request in 1847 and eight years later stated in a solemn declaration:

> We declare, pronounce and define that the doctrine which holds that the Blessed Virgin Mary at the first instant of her conception, by a singular privilege and grace of the Omnipotent God, in virtue of the merits of Jesus Christ, the Savior of mankind, was preserved immaculate from all stain of original sin, has been revealed by God, and therefore should firmly and constantly be believed by all the faithful.

The popular forms of devotion to the Immaculate Conception of Mary can be traced to two apparitions of the Blessed Virgin Mary. The first took place in 1830, when the Blessed Virgin appeared to Sister Catherine Labouré and asked that a medal be struck bearing the inscription "O Mary, conceived without sin, pray for us who have recourse to you." This medal became known as the Miraculous Medal.

The other event was the apparition of Mary to the peasant girl Bernadette Soubirous in 1858, four years after the Holy Father's infallible decree was issued. Commanded by the clergy to seek some proof that this was indeed the Blessed Virgin Mary, Bernadette had asked the Lady of the vision for something to convince them. In response to this plea, Bernadette received a simple but profound statement from the Blessed Mother: "I am the Immaculate Conception."

This message of the Virgin convinced those clergymen who could not believe that a simple peasant girl would have any way of knowing such a complex theological term. The subsequent miracles that have occurred at Lourdes, where St. Bernadette heard the Lady proclaim her title, and the pope's infallible decree have helped spread devotion to Mary's Immaculate Conception throughout the world.

Novena in Honor of the Immaculate Conception

(The following prayers are repeated once a day for nine consecutive days.)

Opening Prayers

Almighty Father, we offer this novena to honor the Blessed Virgin Mary. She occupies a place in the Church, which is highest after Christ and yet very close to us, for You chose her to give to the world that very Life which renews all things, Jesus Christ, Your Son and Our Lord.

And so we praise you, Mary, virgin and mother. After the Savior Himself, you alone are holy, free from all stain of sin, gifted by God from the first instant of your conception with a unique holiness.

We praise and honor you.

Mary, free from all sin and led by the Holy Spirit, you embraced God's saving will with a full heart, and devoted yourself totally as a handmaid of the Lord to the fulfillment of His will in your life, and to the mystery of man's redemption.

We thank you and love you.

Mary, your privileged and grace-filled origin is the Father's final step in preparing humanity to receive its Redeemer in human form. Your fullness of grace is the Father's sign of His favor to the Church and also His promise to the Church of its perfection as the Bride of Christ, radiant in beauty. Your holiness in the beginning of your life is the foreshadowing of that all-embracing holiness with which the

Father will surround His people when His Son comes at the end of time to greet us.

We bless you among all women.

Mary, we turn with confidence to you who are always ready to listen with a mother's affection and powerful assistance. Consoler of the Afflicted, Health of the Sick, Refuge of Sinners, grant us comfort in tribulation, relief in sickness, and liberating strength in our weakness. You, who are free from sin, lead us to combat sin. Obtain for us the victory of hope over anguish, of fellowship over alienation, of peace over anxiety, of joy and beauty over boredom and disgust, of eternal visions over temporal ones, of life over death. O Mary, conceived without sin, pray for us who have recourse to you.

(Mention your request here.)

Let us pray:

God Our Father, we make these petitions through Mary. We pray most especially for the coming of Your kingdom. May You, together with Your Son and Holy Spirit, be known, loved, and glorified and Your law of love faithfully followed. We pray in faith through Jesus Christ, Your Son and Our Lord, in whom all fullness dwells, now and forever. Amen.

Act of Consecration

Most Holy Trinity: Our Father in heaven, who chose Mary as the fairest of Your daughters; Holy Spirit, who chose Mary as Your spouse; God the Son, who chose Mary as Your Mother; in union with Mary, we adore Your majesty and acknowledge Your supreme eternal dominion and authority.

Most Holy Trinity, we put the United States of America into the hands of Mary Immaculate in order that she may present the country to You. Through her we wish to thank You for the great resources of this land and for the freedom which has been its heritage. Through the intercession of Mary, have mercy on the Catholic Church in America. Grant us peace. Have mercy on our president and on all the officers of our government. Grant us a fruitful economy born of justice and charity. Have mercy on capital and industry and labor. Protect the family life of the nation. Guard the innocence of our children. Grant the precious gift of many religious vocations. Through the intercession of our Mother, have mercy on the sick, the poor, the tempted, sinners — on all who are in need.

Mary, Immaculate Virgin, our Mother, Patroness of our land, we praise you and honor you and give ourselves to you. Protect us from every harm. Pray for us, that acting always according to your will and the Will of your Divine Son, we may live and die pleasing to God.

National Shrine of the Immaculate Conception

A national shrine in honor of the patroness of the United States was the dream of Bishop Thomas J. Shanan. The bishop first proposed building the shrine during an audience with Pope St. Pius X on the Feast of the Assumption of Mary in 1913. The Holy Father responded with a personal donation of four hundred dollars and called on Catholics in the United States to support this worthy cause.

Soon donations began to pour in, and the bishop appointed Father Bernard McKenna as the first director of the shrine. On September 23, 1920, the archbishop of Baltimore, James Cardinal Gibbons, blessed the foundation stone for the shrine. Shortly after it began, work on the shrine was delayed by the Great Depression and the Second World War.

When the war was over, Archbishop John Noll (the founder of Our Sunday Visitor) of Fort Wayne, Indiana, and Patrick Cardinal Boyle of Washington, D.C., revived the effort to complete the national shrine. During the Marian Year of 1954, Catholics throughout the United States responded generously and work on the shrine resumed. The shrine was dedicated on November 20, 1959.

The shrine is one of the largest churches in the world, and its more than sixty chapels and oratories represent the diversity of Catholics in the United States.

Basilica of the National Shrine of the Immaculate Conception
400 Michigan Avenue Northeast
Washington, DC 20017-1566
Telephone: 202-526-8300
E-mail: info@nationalshrine.com
Website: http://www.nationalshrine.com/

CHAPTER 6
Our Lady of La Leche

Our Lady of the Milk and Happy Delivery

History of the Devotion

Devotion to the Blessed Virgin Mary under the title of Our Lady of La Leche, referring to her role in nursing the Christ Child, can be traced back to the Milk Grotto in Bethlehem in the fourth century. The grotto commemorates a place where tradition tells us that the Holy Family's flight into Egypt to escape Herod's wrath was delayed so that the Blessed Virgin could nurse the Holy Infant. The legend relates that while nursing the Child, Mary spilled some breast milk on the ground, turning all of the surrounding rock white. The story goes on to say that St. Paula, who lived in Bethlehem in the late fourth century, built a church on the spot.

After the Franciscans took custody of the church in the fourteenth century, white stones from the grotto were exported to various churches throughout Europe under the name of "The Virgin's Milk." The Crusaders brought the devotion back to Spain with them.

During the reign of King Philip III of Spain in 1598, a nobleman, whose wife was about to give birth, feared that she would die. The young couple turned to the intercession of Nuestra Señora de la Leche y Buen Parto (Spanish for "Our Lady of the Milk and Happy Delivery"), whose statue they had enthroned in their home. The mother and child both survived and as a result devotion to Mary under this title spread throughout Spain.

The devotion spread to the Spanish colonies when the Spanish settlers of what today is Florida established a church at the Mission of the Name of God and placed it under the patronage of Our Lady of La Leche. They built the small mission church on the very spot where the first Mass had been celebrated in the United States on the Feast of the Birth of Mary, September 8, 1565.

Novena to Our Lady of La Leche

(The following prayer is repeated once a day for nine consecutive days.)

Lovely Lady of La Leche, most loving mother of Jesus, and my mother, listen to my humble prayer. Your motherly heart knows my every wish, my every need. To you only, His spotless Virgin Mother, has your Divine Son given to understand the sentiments which fill my soul. Yours was the sacred privilege of being the mother of the Savior. Intercede with Him now, my loving mother, that in accordance with His will *(mention your request here)*. This I ask, O Lady of La Leche, in the name of your Divine Son, my Lord and Redeemer. Amen.

Our Lady of La Leche, pray for us.

Shrine of Our Lady of La Leche

A 208-foot stainless steel cross marks the spot where Pedro Menéndez de Avilés knelt to kiss the wooden cross presented him by Father Francisco López de Mendoza Grajales as he claimed the New World for Spain and the Church on September 8, 1565. The towering new cross was erected in 1966 by Archbishop Joseph P. Hurley to mark the four hundredth anniversary of the planting of the cross on American soil.

The first shrine ever established and dedicated to the Virgin Mary in the U.S. was built in St. Augustine, Florida, in 1620 by Spanish settlers and indigenous peoples who had been converted to the faith. There have been several chapels built on the present spot. The first was probably destroyed by fire. The second was razed by the Spanish, who feared the British would use it as a vantage point to attack the nearby fort. The third chapel was destroyed by a hurricane. The present chapel was built in 1914 and was recently renovated in 1988 during the Marian Year.

The shrine grounds contain many interesting and historical artifacts, including some ongoing archeological digs. The gigantic cross on the grounds is surrounded by various Marian shrines that illustrate the seven sorrows of Mary from various ethnic expressions. The statue of Our Lady of La Leche enshrined in the Mission Church is a replica of the original. Expectant mothers come to the shrine begging Mary's intercession for a safe delivery of their child.

Mission of Nombre de Dios
Shrine of Our Lady of La Leche
30 Ocean Avenue
St. Augustine, FL 32804
Telephone: 904-824-3045
E-mail: mission@aug.com
Website: http://userpages.aug.com/mission/index.html

CHAPTER 7

Our Lady of the Miraculous Medal

"O Mary, conceived without sin, pray for us who have recourse to you."

History of the Devotion

Z oé, the ninth of seventeen children of Pierre Labouré and Madeleine Louise Gontard, was born on May 2, 1806. The Labourés were farmers, and young Zoé received no formal education. She is said to have exhibited a deep love for the

Eucharist and attended daily Mass at a time when to do so was not a common practice. Shortly after Zoé's ninth birthday, her mother died. A few years later, her older sister Louise left home for religious life, leaving Zoé, at the age of twelve, in charge of the household and taking care of her father and siblings.

When she was twenty-two, Zoé was sent by her father to an uncle in Paris who owned a café. There she worked as a waitress. Within a few years she left this job in order to pursue the religious vocation she had desired since childhood. She joined St. Vincent de Paul's Daughters of Charity in Paris in January of 1830 at the age of twenty-three. It was here that Zoé was given the name Catherine in religion.

Shortly after entering the Daughters of Charity, Catherine Labouré had several experiences in which the heart of St. Vincent de Paul appeared over a reliquary containing the saint's relics. Catherine also found that Christ was visible to her when she gazed upon the Blessed Sacrament during Mass. She kept all these mystical experiences to herself, sharing them only with her spiritual director under holy obedience.

On the night of July19, Catherine was awakened by what she described as a shining child who beckoned her to come to the chapel. At first she was reluctant to go, fearing that she would be observed, but the glowing child was persistent. When she followed the child into the chapel, she found the Blessed Virgin Mary sitting in the chair of the Mother Superior.

The child whispered in Catherine's ear that the Blessed Virgin wished to speak to her. Catherine approached the Virgin and knelt at her feet, resting her hands in Mary's lap. The Blessed Virgin conversed with Catherine for the next two hours. She confided in Catherine that God had a special mission for her to fulfill; she also foretold the violent death of the archbishop of Paris (which in fact happened forty years later) and the end of the monarchy in France. Just as Catherine and the

Blessed Mother ended their conversation, the luminescent child reappeared and led Catherine back to the dormitory.

The next vision occurred in November of the same year when she was with the other nuns in the convent chapel for the evening meditation. While praying, Catherine heard the rustling of clothing in the air. Looking up toward the altar, she saw the Blessed Virgin standing on a globe. Brilliant light flowed from the hands of Mary, eventually obliterating the globe that she stood on. Words surrounded the Virgin: "O Mary, conceived without sin, pray for us who have recourse to you."

At this point the Virgin spoke to Catherine requesting that a medal be struck in the image she had just witnessed. The design for the back of the medal appeared as a large M with a cross through it, along with two hearts, symbolizing Jesus' entry into this world through Mary. Catherine asked the Virgin how she was to accomplish this mission. Mary told her to relate all to her confessor, who would see that the task came to completion.

Catherine did as she had been told, but her confessor, Father Jean Marie Aladel, was reluctant to believe her. She persisted in her story and after two years Father Aladel went to the archbishop of Paris and obtained permission to have the medal struck. The medal and devotion to the Immaculate Conception of Mary spread quickly throughout France and eventually throughout the world.

Catherine herself lived in relative obscurity in the convent, taking care of the elderly. Her fellow nuns had no idea that she had been the recipient of the visions of the Miraculous Medal until she revealed this to them a few months before her death in 1876. Catherine Labouré's incorrupt body lies in the chapel where the Blessed Virgin appeared and made known the design of the Miraculous Medal. She was canonized in 1947.

Novena to Our Lady of the Miraculous Medal

(The following prayers are repeated once a day for nine consecutive days.)

Prayer to the Holy Spirit*

O Mary, conceived without sin, pray for us who have recourse to you.

Novena Prayers

Lord Jesus Christ, who have glorified your mother, the Blessed Virgin Mary, immaculate from the first moment of her conception, grant that all who devoutly implore her protection on earth may eternally enjoy your presence in heaven. Lord Jesus Christ, who for the accomplishment of your greatest works have chosen the weak things of the world, that no flesh may glory in your sight, and who for a better and more widely diffused belief in the Immaculate Conception of your Mother, have wished that the Miraculous Medal be manifested to St. Catherine Labouré, grant, we ask you, that filled with like humility, we may glorify this mystery by word and work. Amen.

Immaculate Virgin Mary, mother of our Lord Jesus and our mother, we have confidence in your powerful and never-failing intercession, manifested often through the Miraculous Medal. We, your loving and trustful children, ask you to

---

obtain for us the graces and favors we ask during this novena if they will be for the glory of God and the salvation of souls *(mention your request here)*. You know, O Mary, how often our souls have been the sanctuaries of your Son who hates iniquity. Obtain for us then a deep hatred of sin and that purity of heart which will attach us to God alone so that our every thought, word, and deed may tend to his greater glory. Obtain for us also a spirit of prayer and self-denial that we may recover by penance what we have lost by sin and at length attain to that blessed abode where you are the queen of angels and of men. Amen.

Prayer to Our Lady of the Miraculous Medal

Virgin Mother of God, Mary Immaculate, we unite ourselves to you under your title of Our Lady of the Miraculous Medal. May this medal be for each one of us a sure sign of your motherly affection for us and a constant reminder of our filial duties toward you. While wearing it, may we be blessed by your loving protection and preserved in the grace of your Son. Most powerful Virgin, Mother of our Savior, keep us close to you every moment of our lives so that like you we may live and act according to the teaching and example of your Son. Obtain for us, your children, the grace of a happy death so that in union with you we may enjoy the happiness of heaven forever. Amen.

O Mary, conceived without sin, pray for us who have recourse to you.

(Pray the Memorare.*)

---

*The "Memorare" can be found in the "Prayers Common to Novenas," p. 252.

National Shrine of Our Lady of the Miraculous Medal

The church that houses the Shrine of Our Lady of the Miraculous Medal was founded by a group of Vincentian missionaries sent from Bardstown, Kentucky, in 1818. The first church was a simple log cabin that is still preserved at the shrine today. The foundation for the present church was laid in 1827 and was built largely through the generosity of the European benefactors.

The shrine chapel was built on the hundredth anniversary of the first apparition of the Blessed Virgin to St. Catherine Labouré in Rue du Bac, Paris, in 1930. The first superior of the Vincentians in the United States, Venerable Felix de Andreis, is buried in the church close to the shrine of the Miraculous Medal.

The Association of the Miraculous Medal
1811 West St. Joseph Street
Perryville, MO 63775-1598
Telephone: 1-800-264-6279 (toll-free) or 1-573-547-8344
E-mail: ammfather@amm.org
Website: http://www.amm.org/

CHAPTER 8
Our Lady of Monte Cassino

"Our life, our sweetness, and our hope."

History of the Devotion

In 1853, Benedictine monks arrived in southern Indiana to establish a monastery that would serve the local population and eventually train priests. About a mile from where the monks established the monastery was a hill where the students and monks would go for recreation and retreat. One of the monks, Father Chrysostom Foffa, O.S.B., nicknamed the site Monte Cassino, after the monastery where St. Benedict established Western monasticism.

During a visit in 1857, one of monks attached an image of Mary's Immaculate Conception on a tree, thereby establishing the first Marian shrine at the site. A year later, seminary students from the monastery built a wooden chapel to house this image. Ten years later, in 1867, when sandstone was being excavated from the nearby quarry for the construction of a new monastery, the superior of the community decided that the first stones would be set aside for a permanent chapel. At the same time, an image was being carved in Switzerland to be placed over the altar in the new shrine.

The shrine with the new image was dedicated in May of 1870. The statue of Mary holding the infant Jesus in her lap was blessed and enshrined in a spot over the altar where it remains to this day.

Toward the end of 1871, there was an outbreak of small-pox both in the village of St. Meinrad and at the monastery and seminary. Several people died while more were getting sick with each passing day.

On January 5, 1872, those students who were well enough to make the mile journey walked to the shrine and began a novena imploring Our Lady of Monte Cassino to intercede for an end to the outbreak. They repeated this act for the next nine days. The disease stopped spreading on the first day of the novena. Since then, it has been the custom for representatives of the seminary community to make a pilgrimage each year on or about January 13 in thanksgiving for Our Lady of Monte Cassino's intercession.

In 1886, five-year-old Alphonse Bedel, suffering from a

hip disease, was brought to the shrine by his parents. The child, who was unable to walk, was placed before the image of Our Lady and a short while later left the shrine, walking along happily with his parents.

Novena to Our Lady of Monte Cassino

(The following prayer is repeated once a day for nine consecutive days.)

Dearest Mother Mary, attracted to you by your goodness, sympathy, and motherliness, and also because of my needs, I come before you today. I love you, dearest Mother, and I pray that I may learn to love you more and more. I ask you to keep me always under your special protection, and to help me in all my needs, especially for *(mention your request here)*. Please listen with love to the prayers and petitions of all who come to your shrine to seek your aid and to honor you. Also, obtain for each one of us through your powerful intercession with Jesus, your Son, all the graces we need to lead good lives and follow His teachings, especially His command to love one another. Amen.

Our Lady of Monte Cassino, pray for us.
St. Benedict, pray for us.
St. Meinrad, pray for us.

Shrine of Our Lady of Monte Cassino

The Shrine of Our Lady of Monte Cassino is located one mile from the Benedictine Archabbey of St. Meinrad. The small shrine church sits nestled at the edge of a forest. The quarry directly behind provided the first stones for the shrine edifice and the massive monastic structure a mile away.

The shrine is open year-round during daylight hours and may be reached either by car or foot from the nearby monastery. Special services are held on Sunday afternoons in May and October when pilgrims gather to listen to a sermon on the Blessed Virgin Mary preached by one of the Benedictine monks and then pray together.

Monte Cassino Shrine
St. Meinrad Archabbey
St. Meinrad, IN 47577-1010
Telephone: 812-357-6585
Website: http://www.saintmeinrad.edu/abbey/shrine.htm

CHAPTER 9

Our Lady of Mount Carmel

"Whoever dies wearing this scapular shall not suffer eternal fire."

History of the Devotion

Mount Carmel was the destination of Elisha the prophet when he was jeered by a group of young boys who called out to him, "Go away, baldhead! Go away, baldhead!" (2 Kings

2:23). The prophet, obviously not in a good mood on this day, cursed the boys and a few moments later two bears came out of the woods and mauled the group. The Scripture then says that Elisha went to Mount Carmel for a while. The place became hallowed because of the great prophet's presence there and his experience of God.

The Order of Carmelites seems to have its origins in the groups of hermits who lived in caves where Elisha was believed to have stayed during his earlier visit to Mount Carmel. One such follower of this way of life was a man named Simon. Although the stories about him are many, the veracity of most of them is questioned today.

Simon was born in England around 1165 and, as far as we know, lived the normal life of an English lad of that time. It seems that at the age of twelve he retired to the forest where, desiring to live as a hermit, he dwelt in a hollowed-out tree trunk. This earned him the name Simon Stock. At some point during this experience of solitude, he met a group of religious traveling in the area who greatly inspired him and he took leave of the forest to join them.

Next to nothing is known about Simon during this period of his life except that he was noted both for his austerity and holiness. One story recounts how Simon, a strict vegetarian, was offered a dish of cooked fish. Simon became angry and ordered the fish to be thrown back into the river. The waiter did as he had been ordered and the fish miraculously swam away.

When Simon was elected to head the Carmelites, the order had spread throughout Europe but was facing the difficulty of not being accepted by the clergy of various regions, who were wary of new religious groups. Simon and his fellow friars petitioned the Blessed Virgin to assist them in their plight for acceptance in the Church, and Mary responded by gracing Simon with a vision.

She told Simon to entrust his problem with the reigning pontiff and all would be taken care of. She further assured him that all who wore the scapular of the Carmelites to their death would be saved. This message gave the Carmelites confidence that their way of life was righteous and a sure way to attain salvation. It also had the effect of assuring the suspicious clergy outside of their number that God was confirming through this special grace the orthodoxy of the Carmelite Order. (A scapular is part of a religious habit, a piece of cloth that is draped over the front and back of a friar's clothing and worn like an apron.)

The message spread and various popes approved the Carmelites and this Marian devotion. Soon others who were not Carmelites wanted a share in the blessing of Our Lady's promise to Simon. Royal benefactors such as King Edward II of England are said to have worn the scapular of the Carmelites to their grave in hopes of sharing in the promise bestowed on them by Mary. Soon a simplified scapular was constructed, which consisted of two pieces of brown cloth attached by two strings and worn over the head in the manner that the religious scapular would be worn. One of the brown swatches usually has a picture of Our Lady of Mount Carmel holding the Christ Child and handing St. Simon Stock the scapular; on the other piece is often this promise: "Whoever dies wearing this scapular shall not suffer eternal fire."

The scapular is meant to signify a person's commitment to a life lived in perfect obedience to Jesus Christ. The promise attached by Our Lady of Mount Carmel is not a magic formula. Although popular piety has always understood that no magic is involved, there are countless stories of the impious trying to use the scapular as a way to enter heaven cheaply, only to have the scapular ripped from them at the last moment. The tales may be severe, but they point to a reality: the cloth symbolizes a commitment to Jesus in imitation of his mother.

The person receiving the scapular should acknowledge that it is a sacramental of the Church, agree to assimilate the Carmelite Order's spirituality, and embrace the Blessed Virgin Mary as one's loving mother.

Simon Stock died at an advanced age and, although never formally canonized, is considered a saint and has been venerated as one for a very long time. His feast day is celebrated on May 16.

Novena to Our Lady of Mount Carmel

FIRST DAY

(The following prayer, Flos Carmeli [Latin for "Flower of Carmel"], was composed by St. Simon Stock, and in answer he received the scapular from Our Blessed Mother.)

O Beautiful Flower of Carmel, most fruitful vine, splendor of heaven, holy and singular, who brought forth the Son of God, still ever remaining a pure virgin, assist us in our necessity! O Star of the Sea, help and protect us! Show us that you are our Mother!

(Mention your request here.)
Our Father; Hail Mary; Glory Be
Our Lady of Mount Carmel, pray for us.

SECOND DAY

Most Holy Mary, our Mother, in your great love for us you gave us the holy scapular of Mount Carmel, having heard the prayers of your chosen son St. Simon Stock. Help us now to wear it faithfully and with devotion. May it be a sign to us of our desire to grow in holiness.

(Mention your request here.)
Our Father; Hail Mary; Glory Be
Our Lady of Mount Carmel, pray for us.

THIRD DAY

O Queen of Heaven, you gave us the scapular as an outward sign by which we might be known as your faithful children. May we always wear it with honor by avoiding sin and imitating your virtues. Help us to be faithful to this desire of ours.

(Mention your request here.)
Our Father; Hail Mary; Glory Be
Our Lady of Mount Carmel, pray for us.

FOURTH DAY

When you gave us, Gracious Lady, the scapular as our habit, you called us to be not only servants, but also your own children. We ask you to gain for us from your Son the grace to live as your children in joy, peace, and love.

(Mention your request here.)
Our Father; Hail Mary; Glory Be
Our Lady of Mount Carmel, pray for us.

FIFTH DAY

O Mother of Fair Love, through your goodness, as your children, we are called to live in the spirit of Carmel. Help us to live in charity with one another, prayerful as Elijah of old, and mindful of our call to minister to God's people.

(Mention your request here.)
Our Father; Hail Mary; Glory Be
Our Lady of Mount Carmel, pray for us.

SIXTH DAY

With loving provident care, O Mother Most Amiable, you covered us with your scapular as a shield of defense against the Evil One. Through your assistance, may we bravely struggle against the powers of evil, always open to your Son, Jesus Christ.

(Mention your request here.)
Our Father; Hail Mary; Glory Be
Our Lady of Mount Carmel, pray for us.

SEVENTH DAY

O Mary, Help of Christians, you assured us that wearing your scapular worthily would keep us safe from harm. Protect us in both body and soul with your continual aid. May all that we do be pleasing to your Son and to you.

(Mention your request here.)
Our Father; Hail Mary; Glory Be
Our Lady of Mount Carmel, pray for us.

EIGHTH DAY

You give us hope, O Mother of Mercy, that through your scapular promise we might quickly pass through the fires of purgatory to the kingdom of your Son. Be our comfort and our hope. Grant that our hope may not be in vain but that, ever faithful to your Son and to you, we may speedily enjoy after death the blessed company of Jesus and the saints.

(Mention your request here.)
Our Father; Hail Mary; Glory Be
Our Lady of Mount Carmel, pray for us.

NINTH DAY

O Most Holy Mother of Mount Carmel, when asked by a saint to grant privileges to the family of Carmel, you gave assurance of your motherly love and help to those faithful to you and to your Son. Behold us, your children. We glory in wearing your holy habit, which makes us members of your family of Carmel, through which we shall have your powerful protection in life, at death, and even after death. Look down with love, O Gate of Heaven, on all those now in their last agony! Look down graciously, O Virgin, Flower of Carmel, on all those in need of help! Look down mercifully, O Mother of our Savior, on all those who do not know that they are numbered among your children. Look down tenderly, O Queen of All Saints, on the poor souls!

(Mention your request here.)
Our Father; Hail Mary; Glory Be
Our Lady of Mount Carmel, pray for us.

National Shrine of Our Lady of Mount Carmel

The National Shrine of Our Lady of Mount Carmel was founded in 1940 to foster and spread devotion to the Blessed Virgin under her Carmelite title along with the Brown Scapular. The original shrine was located in the Carmelite Church of Our Lady of the Scapular of Mount Carmel in New York City. The early apostolate of the shrine was to supply scapulars for men serving in the armed forces who were fighting World War II. The apostolate grew to include workshops on devotion to Mary, the availability of confessions, and the celebration of novenas and Masses.

In 1990, the site of the shrine was transferred to Middletown, New York, where the spacious facility offers the perfect setting for pilgrimage and prayer. Services are held regularly in both English and Spanish, and all are invited to walk in the footsteps of the Blessed Virgin Mary, the model of all Carmelites.

National Shrine of Our Lady of Mount Carmel
P.O. Box 868
Carmelite Drive
Middletown, NY 10940-0868
Telephone: 914-343-1879
E-mail: nsolmc@frontiernet.net
Website: http://www.frontiernet.net/~ocarmvoc/nsolmc.html

CHAPTER 10
Our Lady of Perpetual Help

"Pray for us, that we may be made worthy of the promises of Christ."

History of the Devotion

The origin of the icon that is at the center of devotion to Our Lady of Perpetual Help is unknown. Many have thought that St. Luke painted it, but its existence prior to the late Middle

Ages cannot be confirmed. Likely it is Eastern in origin because of the Byzantine style and Greek lettering. The icon shows the Child Jesus fleeing into his mother's protective arms as the archangels Michael and Gabriel show him the instruments of crucifixion. The Greek letters spell out the first letters of Mary's and Jesus' names.

The icon arrived in Rome in the fifteenth century after a merchant who had heard about a miraculous image in the island of Crete went to the island and stole it. When he arrived in Rome with the icon among his wares, he fell very ill. As he lay dying, he ordered that a friend place the icon in a church, perhaps hoping that it would alleviate his suffering. The friend took the icon to his own home where his wife hung it in their bedroom.

The Virgin, evidently not pleased with this arrangement, appeared several times to the man and told him she wanted her image to be placed in a church. The man, despite the miraculous visitation, was not moved to relinquish control of the image. The Blessed Virgin next appeared to the man's daughter and asked that the icon be enshrined in a church between the two relatively huge churches of St. Mary Major and St. John Lateran. The daughter communicated this to her father and he relented; thus the icon was enshrined in 1499 in St. Matthew's, the church that lies between the two larger edifices.

Pilgrims flocked to the small church for three hundred years to pray before the miraculous image, until Napoleon's invading army destroyed the church in 1798. Once the soldiers had left the area, people searched the ruins looking for the image but could not locate it anywhere. It seemed that the image had been lost and for the next sixty years there was no mention of it.

In 1855, the Order of Redemptorists came to Rome and its members were granted possession of the location where St.

Matthew's had once stood to build a church in honor of their founder, St. Alphonsus Liguori. It happened that a young Redemptorist priest remembered that as a young boy he had been told of a miraculous image that had once been enshrined in the previous church. The image had been safely transferred to an Augustinian monastery near Rome.

When the Redemptorists heard of this, they petitioned the pope to allow the image to be returned to the spot that the Blessed Virgin had requested. The Holy Father granted their request and further commissioned the Redemptorist Order to spread devotion to Our Lady of Perpetual Help throughout the world. The image was transferred in a solemn procession on April 26, 1866, to the Church of St. Alphonsus.

Today replicas of the image of Our Lady of Perpetual Help grace the altars of countless churches throughout the world.

Novena to Our Lady of Perpetual Help

(The following prayers are repeated once a day for nine consecutive days.)

Behold at your feet, O Mother of Perpetual Help, a wretched sinner who has recourse to you and confides in you. O Mother of Mercy, have pity on me. I hear you called by all, the Refuge and the Hope of sinners; be, then, my refuge and my hope. Assist me, for the love of Jesus Christ; stretch forth your hand to a miserable fallen creature, who recommends himself to you, and who devotes himself to your service forever. I bless and thank Almighty God, who in His mercy has given me this confidence in you, which I hold to be a pledge of my eternal salvation. It is true, dearest Mother, that in the past I have miserably fallen into sin, because I had not turned to you. I know that with your help, I shall conquer. I know, too, that you will assist me, if I recommend myself to you; but I fear, dear Mother, that in time of danger, I may neglect to call on you, and thus lose my soul. This grace, then, I ask of you with all the fervor of my soul, that, in all the attacks of hell, I may ever have recourse to you. O Mary, help me; O Mother of Perpetual Help, never suffer me to lose my God.

Hail Mary *(three times)*

Mother of Perpetual Help, grant that I may ever invoke your most powerful name, which is the safeguard of the living and the salvation of the dying. O Purest Mary, O Sweetest Mary, let your name henceforth be ever on my lips. Delay not, O Blessed Lady, to help me whenever I call on you; for, in all my temptations, in all my needs, I shall never cease to call on you, ever repeating your Sacred Name, Mary! O, what consolation, what sweetness, what confidence, what emotion fills my soul when I utter your Sacred Name, or even only think of you! I thank the Lord for having given you, for my good, so sweet, so powerful, so lovely a name. But I will not be content with merely uttering your name; let my love for you prompt me ever to hail you, Mother of Perpetual Help.

Hail Mary *(three times)*

Mother of Perpetual Help, you are the dispenser of all the gifts which God grants to us miserable sinners; and for this end He has made you so powerful, so rich, and so bountiful, in order that you may help us in our misery. You are the advocate of the most wretched and abandoned sinners who have recourse to you; come to my aid, dearest Mother, for I recommend myself to you. In your hands I place my eternal salvation, and to you I entrust my soul. Count me among your most devoted servants; take me under your protection, and it is enough for me. For, if you protect me, dear Mother, I fear nothing; not from my sins, because you will obtain for me the pardon of them from Jesus your Divine Son. But one thing I fear, that in the hour of temptation, I may through negligence fail to have recourse to you and thus perish miserably. Obtain for me, therefore, the pardon of my sins, love for Jesus, final perseverance, and the grace to have recourse to you and *(mention your request here)*, O Mother of Perpetual Help.

Hail Mary *(three times)*

Pray for us, O Mother of Perpetual Help, that we may be made worthy of the promises of Christ.

Let us pray:

Lord Jesus Christ, who gave us Your Holy Mother Mary, whose renowned image we venerate, to be a Mother ever ready to help us, grant, we beseech You, that we who constantly implore her maternal aid may merit to enjoy perpetually the fruits of Your redemption, who lives and reigns with God forever and ever. Amen.

Basilica of Our Lady
of Perpetual Help

Shortly after the miraculous image of Our Lady of Perpetual Help was restored to the Church of St. Alphonsus in Rome, copies of the image were commissioned. One of these early paintings was sent to the Redemptorists at Our Lady of Perpetual Help Church in Boston, Massachusetts. They enthroned the image above the main altar of their church on Pentecost Sunday of 1871.

Miracles were reported within two days. A child who had an incurable wound was brought before the image and was completely healed. A woman who suffered with palsy approached one of the Redemptorists, who pointed to the image of Our Lady. The woman prayed and found herself miraculously cured. The crowds that soon followed necessitated the building of an even larger church, which is the present-day basilica, in 1878.

Since then, literally hundreds of cures have been attributed to the miraculous image enshrined at the basilica. Crutches left behind by those who were cured rise like flowers in sweet testimony of the healing love experienced there.

Basilica of Our Lady of Perpetual Help
Mission Church
1545 Tremont Street
Boston, MA 02120
Telephone: 617-445-2600
Website: http://themissionchurch.com

CHAPTER 11

Our Lady of Prompt Succor

"Make haste to help us."

History of the Devotion

Agathe Françoise Gensoul was forced to conceal her Ursuline vocation after she and the other nuns of the Convent of Pont-Saint-Esprit were forced out of their religious community by the revolutionary government of late eighteenth-century France. She could no longer use her religious name, Mother St. Michel, but she did strive to continue to live out her vocation as an Ursuline nun by starting a school along with another Ursuline, Sophie Ricard. It was at this time that she received a summons from her cousin, also an Ursuline, in New Orleans, asking that Agathe come to Louisiana.

The city of New Orleans had recently been under Spanish rule, and when it reverted back to French rule the Spanish Ursulines left for Spain, fearing that the terrors against the religious in France would come with French rule to New Orleans. This left the Ursuline convent understaffed.

Mother St. Michel applied directly to the bishop, requesting the transfer to New Orleans. The bishop, faced with the devastation of post-revolutionary France, refused her request, saying that only the pope could authorize such a move. This was effectively closing the book on the matter, as the distance and ability to communicate with the pope in Rome (who was under house arrest at the time) was next to impossible.

Undeterred, Mother St. Michel wrote to Pope Pius VII, repeating her request for permission to go to New Orleans. Three months after she had written the letter, she still had not found a way to send it.

One day while praying before a statue of Mary, Mother St. Michel felt a prompting to pray, "O Most Holy Virgin Mary, if you obtain a prompt and favorable answer to my letter, I promise to have you honored in New Orleans under the title of Our Lady of Prompt Succor."

She not only found a way to send the letter a few days afterward, but a letter dated a month later gave her an answer, very prompt for the communication system of the day. The pope approved and blessed her new undertaking. The bishop was so surprised at this turn of events that he asked to bless the statue that Mother St. Michel was having carved to take with her to New Orleans.

The statue of Our Lady of Prompt Succor was installed in the Ursuline convent in New Orleans on December 30, 1810. A few years later, another miracle would be attributed to the Virgin under this title. A terrible fire ravaged the city of New Orleans in 1812, and the wind was rapidly driving it in the direction of the convent of the Ursulines. One of the nuns, Sister St. Anthony, placed a small replica of Our Lady of Prompt Succor in her window that faced the approaching fire, while Mother St. Michel prayed aloud, asking Our Lady for help. Immediately the wind changed direction, averting the fire.

Mary's help has been sought from the shrine ever since, both in time of war (as in the Battle of New Orleans) and during the threat of hurricanes, a persistent danger on the Gulf Coast.

Novena to Our Lady of Prompt Succor

(The following prayers are repeated once a day for nine consecutive days.)

Our Lady of Prompt Succor, you are, after Jesus, our only hope. O Most Holy Virgin, whose merits have raised you high above angel choirs to the very throne of the Eternal and whose foot crushed the head of the infernal serpent, you are strong against the enemies of our salvation. O Mother of God, you are our Mediatrix most kind and loving. Hasten, then, to our help, and as you once saved the city of New Orleans from ravaging flames and our country from an alien foe, do now have pity on our misery, and obtain for us the graces we beg of you. Deliver us from the wiles of Satan, assist us in the many trials which beset our path in this valley of tears, and be to us truly Our Lady of Prompt Succor now and especially at the hour of our death. Amen.

O Mary, Mother of God, who amid the tribulations of the world, watches over us and over the Church of your Son, be to us and to the Church, truly, Our Lady of Prompt Succor; make haste to help us in all our necessities, that in this fleeting life you may be our succor, and obtain for us *(mention your request here)*. Help us to gain life everlasting through the merits of Jesus, your Son, Our Lord and Redeemer. Amen.

National Shrine of Our Lady of Prompt Succor

The Ursuline nuns gave the convent building that housed the original shrine to Bishop Dubourg and his successors as a residence in 1824 before moving into a new facility. That building now houses the Archdiocese of New Orleans archives.

The statue of Our Lady of Prompt Succor that Mother St. Michel brought with her from France is enshrined in the convent chapel. The smaller statue, fondly referred to as "sweetheart," that Sister St. Anthony placed in the window during the fire of 1812 is now on display in the convent museum.

National Votive Shrine of Our Lady of Prompt Succor
2635 State Street
New Orleans, LA 70118
Telephone: 504-866-1472
Website: http://www.gnofn.org/~ursuline/page5.htm

CHAPTER 12

Our Lady of the Snows

"O Mother of the Word Incarnate, despise not my petitions."

History of the Devotion

Two events that converged into a single event are the basis for this devotion that may very well be the oldest continuous devotion to the Blessed Virgin Mary. It involves a pope, a wealthy couple, and the building of a very large church.

It was during the summer of 352, the hottest time of the

year in Rome. Pope Liberius had a very vivid dream in which the Blessed Virgin Mary asked the pontiff to build a church in her honor on a location where snow would fall on the next day.

Meanwhile, also in Rome, an elderly patrician named John and his wife, who had remained childless, had vowed to leave their inheritance to the Blessed Virgin Mary. As the couple slept, they both had the same dream similar to that of Pope Liberius, in which the Blessed Mother was requesting that the couple donate money to build a church in her honor on the hill where the snow would fall.

The next day the couple went to the pope and related the dream that they had experienced the previous night. The Holy Father related that he, too, had shared the dream and went with the couple to discover that the Esquiline Hill was covered with snow even though the temperature outside was in the 90s.

Pope Liberius had the foundation laid for the church, but it was Pope Sixtus, almost one hundred years later, who dedicated the Basilica of St. Mary Major.

The church contains a relic of the crib of the Nativity that either is an early replica or the actual crib of the Child Jesus. A painting, which at times has been attributed to St. Luke and is done on cedar slabs, hangs in the church and is known by the title of Protectress of the Roman People. The church along with the story of Our Lady of Snows is a testament of the early Church's devotion to the Mother of God and her miraculous share in her Son's power.

Interestingly, even though the story refers to an event that happened in a Mediterranean climate during the middle of the summer, devotion to Mary under the title of Our Lady of the Snows has flourished in the lands where snow is no miracle but a fact of life.

Novena to Our Lady of the Snows

(The following prayer is repeated once a day for nine consecutive days.)

Remember, O most gracious Virgin Mary, that never was it known that anyone who fled to your protection, implored your help, or sought your intercession was left unaided. Inspired by this confidence, I fly unto you, O Virgin of virgins, my Mother. To you do I come, before you I stand, sinful and sorrowful. O Mother of the Word Incarnate, despise not my petitions, but in your mercy hear and answer me. Amen.

Our Father; Hail Mary

Our Lady of the Snows, pray for us.
St. Joseph, pray for us.
St. Thérèse, the Little Flower, pray for us.
St Eugene de Mazenod, pray for us.*

Glory Be

---

*St. Eugene de Mazenod, OMI, is the founder of the Missionary Oblates of Mary Immaculate.

Shrine of Our Lady of the Snows

In 1941, Father Edwin J. Guild, a member of the Missionary Oblates of Mary Immaculate, founded the shrine, perhaps the largest outdoor shrine in North America at over two hundred acres. Devotion to Mary under the title of Our Lady of the Snows was introduced in hopes of fostering a sense of prayer and support for the missionaries of the order, many of whom were stationed in the Arctic regions.

The shrine is both traditional and very modern, featuring chapels ablaze with candles, alongside multimedia presentations that would rival any theme park in the country.

National Shrine of Our Lady of the Snows
422 South DeMazenod Drive
Belleville, IL 62223-1094
Telephone: 618-397-6700
Website: http://www.oblatesusa.org/index.html

Part 4

Novenas to the Relatives of Jesus

"Whoever does the will of God is my brother,
and sister, and mother."

MARK 3:35

CHAPTER 13
St. Ann

Mother of the Blessed Virgin Mary, Grandmother of Jesus

History of the Devotion

The parents of the Blessed Virgin Mary are first mentioned in the late second-century apocryphal work called the *Protoevangelium of St. James*. According to that account, a man named Joachim was a shepherd in charge of raising the lambs that were used for the temple sacrifice in Bethlehem.

He was married to Ann but was scorned by his fellow shepherds because the couple was childless after twenty years of marriage, which was considered a curse during Old Testament times.

Joachim, retiring to the desert, cried to God. An angel comforted him with a message that his sorrow was near an end. Ann, who had remained behind in Bethlehem, also received an angelic visitation. The angel told her that God had heard the prayer of the couple and that Ann would conceive and bring forth a child that would be spoken of throughout the world. Ann, for her part, replied to the angel that if such a child, whether male or female, were to be born, she would dedicate it to God's service. The angel had told both Joachim and Ann to go to the Golden Gate in Jerusalem, which they did; there, they rejoiced over the angel's revelation that they would have a child.

Returning home to Bethlehem, the happy couple conceived and bore a daughter whom they named Mary. When the child was three years old, they traveled with her to the Temple in Jerusalem and dedicated the promised child to the Lord. Setting Mary down in front of the Temple, the couple watched as she climbed the fifteen steps up toward the Temple entrance. Ann and Joachim took this as a sign of their young daughter's desire to be close to God.

Devotion to St. Ann, the mother of Mary and grandmother of Jesus, can be dated back to the first shrine dedicated in her honor by Justinian I in the sixth century. Also, there is mention of the saintly parents being included on a vestment presented by Pope Leo III to the Basilica of St. Mary Major in the eighth century.

Another wave of devotion to Ann revolves around the belief that Mary Magdalene and Lazarus had transported her remains to France in the first century. A bishop purportedly had buried the remains in a cave at Apt beneath a church dedicated to the Blessed Virgin. The area had all but been forgotten when the church was destroyed by invaders and left in ruins.

Some six hundred years later, miners uncovered the cave and, discovering the long-lost relics, took St. Ann as their patroness. The church was rebuilt and became a great shrine to St. Ann in Europe during the Middle Ages.

Pope Urban VI granted that a feast be celebrated by the English Church in 1382 after the English Catholics had petitioned for such a feast. The universal Church did not celebrate St. Ann's feast until 1584.

Novena to St. Ann

(The following prayers are repeated once a day for nine consecutive days.)

Sign of the Cross

Incline unto my aid, O God; O Lord, make haste to help me.

Let us pray:
O Almighty God, Father of mercies and Giver of all good gifts, we kneel before You to honor You in Your Saints; and to seek their intercession in our many needs. We are truly sorry for all our sins, and humbly ask Your pardon. Please grant our petitions and a full measure of the indulgences granted by Your Vicar, the pope, and draw us ever nearer to Your Divine Heart. Amen.

Prayer to St. Ann
With a heart full of sincere and filial veneration, I prostrate myself before you, O Blessed St. Ann. You are that beloved and privileged creature who, because of your extraordinary virtue and sanctity, did deserve of God that chief of graces, of giving life to the treasury of grace, the blessed among women, the Mother of the Incarnate Lord, the Blessed Virgin Mary.

In consideration of such exalted favors, please, O most tender saint, receive me among the number of your truly devoted servants, for such I profess myself to be and wish to remain for the rest of my life. Surround me with your efficacious patronage and obtain for me knowledge of my sins and sorrow for them, an ardent love of Jesus and Mary, and a faithful and constant observance of the duties of my state in life. Save me from all dangers in life and assist me at the hour of my death that I may safely reach Paradise, there to praise with you, most happy Mother, the Word of God made man in the womb of your most pure daughter, the Blessed Virgin Mary. Amen.

Our Father; Hail Mary; Glory Be

Prayer to St. Ann to Obtain a Special Favor
O Glorious St. Ann, filled with compassion for those who invoke you and with love for those who suffer, heavily laden with the weight of my troubles, I cast myself at your feet and humbly beg of you to take the present affair which I recommend to you under your special protection *(mention your request here)*. Please recommend it to your daughter, the Blessed Virgin Mary, and lay it before the throne of Jesus so that He may bring it to a happy issue. Please continue to intercede for me until my request is granted. Above all, obtain for me the grace of one day beholding my God face to face and with you and Mary and all the saints praising and blessing Him for all eternity. Amen.

(Say the following prayer three times.)
Good St. Ann, Mother of her who is our life, our sweetness, and our hope, pray to her for us and obtain our requests.

Good St. Ann, pray for us.

Basilica of the National Shrine of St. Ann

In 1905, the Passionists built a monastery over a coal mine in Scranton, Pennsylvania. They dedicated their new home to St. Ann. However, the site they chose began to fall apart on August 15, 1911, due to the collapse of the mines underneath. The priests and brothers had to evacuate but had perfect confidence that through the intercession of their patroness, St. Ann, all would be well. After some repairs, the Passionists once again reclaimed their monastery. In 1913, another disaster loomed when more shifts in the hollow ground beneath the monastery threatened to sweep the edifice right off the hill.

The village of Scranton prayed to St. Ann that this disaster would be averted. The next morning the slide subsided. Devotion to St. Ann developed from these early near tragedies. The Passionists have prayed a weekly novena to the saint since 1905, but the novena became public in 1924. At times, up to seventeen thousand people have attended the novena.

The church was named and dedicated a basilica in 1997.

Basilica of the National Shrine of St. Ann
1239 St. Ann Street
Scranton, PA 18504
Telephone: 570-347-5691
Fax: 570-347-9387
Website: http://visioni.com/~smh/basilica.htm

CHAPTER 14

St. Joseph

Guardian of the Redeemer

History of the Devotion

St. Joseph is the spouse of the Blessed Virgin Mary and the guardian of Jesus. The Gospel of Matthew shows Joseph to be a faith-filled man listening and heeding several times the message of an angel made known to him in a dream. The first time relates to his vocation with respect to the virginal conception of Jesus. An angel in a dream tells Joseph not to fear and to take Mary for his wife and to give the Child a name. The second time relates to the slaughter of the Holy Innocents when Joseph is warned to take Mary and the infant Christ into Egypt for their protection.

We know that he was an artisan by trade and that he was of the royal lineage of King David. Since he is never mentioned as being around when Jesus begins his adult ministry, most believe that Joseph had already died by that time and he is thus considered the patron of a happy death.

Whatever the details of his life, Scripture relates that he was a just man.

Devotion to Joseph has been traced back as far as the fourth century in the Eastern Church where devotion was largely fueled by a work called the *History of Joseph the Carpenter*. It seems to have taken longer to catch on in the West, where the earliest reference to a feast in honor of Joseph is in the eighth century.

Devotion to Joseph has flourished since the sixteenth century, largely due to the influence of St. Teresa of Ávila. She could be called St. Joseph's personal saint, with reference to her diligence in spreading his devotion. In 1870, Pope Pius IX declared St. Joseph the patron of the universal Church. The command of Pharaoh in Genesis to the people of Egypt referring to the earlier patriarch, *Ite ad Ioseph* (Latin for "Go to Joseph"), is often applied to him.

There are currently three universal feasts in honor of St. Joseph. His principal feast, St. Joseph, Husband of the Blessed Virgin Mary, is celebrated on March 19. The Feast of St. Joseph the Worker is May 1. The Feast of the Holy Family is the Sunday within the Christmas Octave, or December 30. The

Oblates of St. Joseph and other religious orders dedicated to honoring St. Joseph celebrate the Feast of the Holy Spouses Mary and Joseph on January 23 each year.

St. Joseph is the patron of the universal Church, the New World, families, workers, unborn children and expectant parents, migrants and refugees, and a peaceful death.

Novena to St. Joseph

Opening Prayer to St. Joseph for Faith

O blessed St. Joseph, heir of all the patriarchs, obtain for me this beautiful and precious virtue. Give me lively faith, which is the foundation of holiness, that faith that triumphs over all the temptations of the world and conquers human respect; a faith that cannot be shaken and that seeks God alone. In imitation of you, make me live by faith and submit my mind and heart to God, so that one day I may behold in heaven what I now firmly believe on earth.

Reading: Matthew 1:18-21 *(New Revised Standard Version)*

Now the birth of Jesus the Messiah took place in this way. When his mother, Mary, had been engaged to Joseph, but before they lived together, she was found to be with child by the Holy Spirit. Her husband Joseph, being a righteous man and unwilling to expose her to public disgrace, planned to dismiss her quietly. But just when he had resolved to do this, an angel of the Lord appeared to him in a dream and said, "Joseph, son of David, do not be afraid to take Mary as your wife, for the child conceived in her is from the Holy Spirit. She will bear a son, and you are to name him Jesus, for he will save his people from their sins."

Decade of St. Joseph Rosary *(consisting of the following)*
Our Father
Repeat the following prayer ten times: "Joseph, son of

David, and husband of Mary; we honor you, guardian of the Redeemer, and we adore the child you named Jesus. St. Joseph, patron of the universal Church, pray with us that we may imitate you in lifelong dedication to the interests of the Savior."

Glory Be

Prayer to St. Joseph

O blessed St. Joseph, tender-hearted father, faithful guardian of Jesus, chaste spouse of the Mother of God, I pray and beseech you to offer God the Father my praise to Him through His divine Son, who died on the cross and rose again to give us sinners new life. Through the holy name of Jesus, pray with us that we may obtain from the eternal Father the favor we ask *(mention your request here)*. We have been unfaithful to the unfailing love of God the Father; beg of Jesus mercy for us. Amid the splendors of God's loving presence, do not forget the sorrows of those who suffer, those who pray, those who weep. By your prayers and those of your most holy Spouse, our Blessed Lady, may the love of Jesus answer our call of confident hope. Amen.

SECOND DAY
Joseph Takes Mary as His Wife

Opening Prayer to St. Joseph for Faith

O blessed St. Joseph, heir of all the patriarchs, obtain for me this beautiful and precious virtue. Give me lively faith, which is the foundation of holiness, that faith that triumphs over all the temptations of the world and conquers human respect; a faith that cannot be shaken and that seeks God alone. In imitation of you, make me live by faith and submit my mind and heart to God, so that one day I may behold in heaven what I now firmly believe on earth.

Reading: Matthew 1:24 *(New Revised Standard Version)*
When Joseph awoke from sleep, he did as the angel of the Lord commanded him; he took Mary as his wife.

Decade of St. Joseph Rosary *(consisting of the following)*
Our Father
Repeat the following prayer ten times: "Joseph, son of David, and husband of Mary; we honor you, guardian of the Redeemer, and we adore the child you named Jesus. St. Joseph, patron of the universal Church, pray with us that we may imitate you in lifelong dedication to the interests of the Savior."
Glory Be

Prayer to St. Joseph
O blessed St. Joseph, tender-hearted father, faithful guardian of Jesus, chaste spouse of the Mother of God, I pray and beseech you to offer God the Father my praise to Him through His divine Son, who died on the cross and rose again to give us sinners new life. Through the holy name of Jesus, pray with us that we may obtain from the eternal Father the favor we ask *(mention your request here)*. We have been unfaithful to the unfailing love of God the Father; beg of Jesus mercy for us. Amid the splendors of God's loving presence, do not forget the sorrows of those who suffer,

141

those who pray, those who weep. By your prayers and those of your most holy Spouse, our Blessed Lady, may the love of Jesus answer our call of confident hope. Amen.

THIRD DAY
The Birth and Naming of Jesus, Son of David

Opening Prayer to St. Joseph for Faith

O blessed St. Joseph, heir of all the patriarchs, obtain for me this beautiful and precious virtue. Give me lively faith, which is the foundation of holiness, that faith that triumphs over all the temptations of the world and conquers human respect; a faith that cannot be shaken and that seeks God alone. In imitation of you, make me live by faith and submit my mind and heart to God, so that one day I may behold in heaven what I now firmly believe on earth.

Reading: Matthew 1:16, 25 *(New Revised Standard Version)*

And Jacob was the father of Joseph the husband of Mary, of whom Jesus was born, who is called the Messiah. . . . [Joseph] had no marital relations with [Mary] until she had borne him a son, and he named him Jesus.

Decade of St. Joseph Rosary *(consisting of the following)*

Our Father

Repeat the following prayer ten times: "Joseph, son of David, and husband of Mary; we honor you, guardian of the Redeemer, and we adore the child you named Jesus. St. Joseph, patron of the universal Church, pray with us that we may imitate you in lifelong dedication to the interests of the Savior."

Glory Be

Prayer to St. Joseph

O blessed St. Joseph, tender-hearted father, faithful guardian of Jesus, chaste spouse of the Mother of God, I pray and beseech you to offer God the Father my praise to Him through His divine Son, who died on the cross and rose again to give us sinners new life. Through the holy name of Jesus, pray with us that we may obtain from the eternal Father the favor we ask *(mention your request here)*. We have been unfaithful to the unfailing love of God the Father; beg of Jesus mercy for us. Amid the splendors of God's loving presence, do not forget the sorrows of those who suffer, those who pray, those who weep. By your prayers and those of your most holy Spouse, our Blessed Lady, may the love of Jesus answer our call of confident hope. Amen.

FOURTH DAY
The Presentation of Jesus, According to the Law of the Lord

Opening Prayer to St. Joseph for Faith

O blessed St. Joseph, heir of all the patriarchs, obtain for me this beautiful and precious virtue. Give me lively faith, which is the foundation of holiness, that faith that triumphs over all the temptations of the world and conquers human respect; a faith that cannot be shaken and that seeks God alone. In imitation of you, make me live by faith and submit my mind and heart to God, so that one day I may behold in heaven what I now firmly believe on earth.

Reading: Luke 2:22-24, 39-40 *(New Revised Standard Version)*

When the time came for their purification according to the law of Moses, they brought [Jesus] up to Jerusalem to present him to the Lord (as it is written in the law of the Lord, "Every firstborn male shall be designated as holy to the Lord"), and they offered a sacrifice according to what is stated in the law of the Lord, "a pair of turtledoves or two young pigeons."

When they had finished everything required by the law of the Lord, they returned to Galilee, to their own town of Nazareth. The child grew and became strong, filled with wisdom; and the favor of God was upon him.

Decade of St. Joseph Rosary *(consisting of the following)*

Our Father

Repeat the following prayer ten times: "Joseph, son of David, and husband of Mary; we honor you, guardian of the Redeemer, and we adore the child you named Jesus. St. Joseph, patron of the universal Church, pray with us that we may imitate you in lifelong dedication to the interests of the Savior."

Glory Be

Prayer to St. Joseph

O blessed St. Joseph, tender-hearted father, faithful guardian of Jesus, chaste spouse of the Mother of God, I pray and beseech you to offer God the Father my praise to Him through His divine Son, who died on the cross and rose again to give us sinners new life. Through the holy name of Jesus, pray with us that we may obtain from the eternal Father the favor we ask *(mention your request here)*. We have been unfaithful to the unfailing love of God the Father; beg of Jesus mercy for us. Amid the splendors of God's loving presence, do not forget the sorrows of those who suffer, those who pray, those who weep. By your prayers and those of your most holy Spouse, our Blessed Lady, may the love of Jesus answer our call of confident hope. Amen.

FIFTH DAY
The Flight into Egypt

Opening Prayer to St. Joseph for Faith

O blessed St. Joseph, heir of all the patriarchs, obtain for me this beautiful and precious virtue. Give me lively faith, which is the foundation of holiness, that faith that triumphs over all the temptations of the world and conquers human respect; a faith that cannot be shaken and that seeks God alone. In imitation of you, make me live by faith and submit my mind and heart to God, so that one day I may behold in heaven what I now firmly believe on earth.

Reading: Matthew 2:13-15 *(New Revised Standard Version)*

Now after [the wise men] had left, an angel of the Lord appeared to Joseph in a dream and said, "Get up, take the child and his mother, and flee to Egypt, and remain there until I tell you; for Herod is about to search for the child and destroy him." Then Joseph got up and took the child and his mother by night, and went to Egypt, and remained there until the death of Herod.

Decade of St. Joseph Rosary *(consisting of the following)*

Our Father

Repeat the following prayer ten times: "Joseph, son of David, and husband of Mary; we honor you, guardian of the Redeemer, and we adore the child you named Jesus. St. Joseph, patron of the universal Church, pray with us that we may imitate you in lifelong dedication to the interests of the Savior."

Glory Be

Prayer to St. Joseph

O blessed St. Joseph, tender-hearted father, faithful guardian of Jesus, chaste spouse of the Mother of God, I pray and beseech you to offer God the Father my praise to Him through His divine Son, who died on the cross and rose again to give us sinners new life. Through the holy name of Jesus, pray with us that we may obtain from the eternal Father the favor we ask *(mention your request here)*. We have been unfaithful to the unfailing love of God the Father; beg of Jesus mercy for us. Amid the splendors of God's loving presence, do not forget the sorrows of those who suffer, those who pray, those who weep. By your prayers and those of your most holy Spouse, our Blessed Lady, may the love of Jesus answer our call of confident hope. Amen.

SIXTH DAY
The Finding in the Temple and the Fatherhood of Joseph

Opening Prayer to St. Joseph for Faith

O blessed St. Joseph, heir of all the patriarchs, obtain for me this beautiful and precious virtue. Give me lively

faith, which is the foundation of holiness, that faith that triumphs over all the temptations of the world and conquers human respect; a faith that cannot be shaken and that seeks God alone. In imitation of you, make me live by faith and submit my mind and heart to God, so that one day I may behold in heaven what I now firmly believe on earth.

Reading: Luke 2:41-52 *(New Revised Standard Version)*

Now every year his parents went to Jerusalem for the festival of the Passover. And when he was twelve years old, they went up as usual for the festival. When the festival was ended and they started to return, the boy Jesus stayed behind in Jerusalem, but his parents did not know it. Assuming that he was in the group of travelers, they went a day's journey. Then they started to look for him among their relatives and friends. When they did not find him, they returned to Jerusalem to search for him. After three days, they found him in the temple, sitting among the teachers, listening to them, and asking them questions. And all who heard him were amazed at his understanding and his answers. When his parents saw him, they were astonished; and his mother said to him, "Child, why have you treated us like this? Look, your Father and I have been searching for you in great anxiety." He said to them, "Why were you searching for me? Did you not know that I must be in my Father's house?" But they did not understand what he said to them. Then he went down with them and came to Nazareth, and was obedient to them. His mother treasured all these things in her heart. And Jesus increased in wisdom and in years, and in divine and human favor.

Decade of St. Joseph Rosary *(consisting of the following)*

Our Father

Repeat the following prayer ten times: "Joseph, son of David, and husband of Mary; we honor you, guardian of the Redeemer, and we adore the child you named Jesus. St. Joseph, patron of the universal Church, pray with us that we may imitate you in lifelong dedication to the interests of the Savior."

Glory Be

Prayer to St. Joseph

O blessed St. Joseph, tender-hearted father, faithful guardian of Jesus, chaste spouse of the Mother of God, I pray and beseech you to offer God the Father my praise to Him through His divine Son, who died on the cross and rose again to give us sinners new life. Through the holy name of Jesus, pray with us that we may obtain from the eternal Father the favor we ask *(mention your request here)*. We have been unfaithful to the unfailing love of God the Father; beg of Jesus mercy for us. Amid the splendors of God's loving presence, do not forget the sorrows of those who suffer, those who pray, those who weep. By your prayers and those of your most holy Spouse, our Blessed Lady, may the love of Jesus answer our call of confident hope. Amen.

SEVENTH DAY
Joseph the Worker

Opening Prayer to St. Joseph for Faith

O blessed St. Joseph, heir of all the patriarchs, obtain for me this beautiful and precious virtue. Give me lively

faith, which is the foundation of holiness, that faith that triumphs over all the temptations of the world and conquers human respect; a faith that cannot be shaken and that seeks God alone. In imitation of you, make me live by faith and submit my mind and heart to God, so that one day I may behold in heaven what I now firmly believe on earth.

Reading: Matthew 13:54-55a *(New Revised Standard Version)*
Jesus came to his hometown and began to teach the people in their synagogue, so that they were astounded and said, "Where did this man get this wisdom and these deeds of power? Is not this the carpenter's son?"

Decade of St. Joseph Rosary *(consisting of the following)*
Our Father
Repeat the following prayer ten times: "Joseph, son of David, and husband of Mary; we honor you, guardian of the Redeemer, and we adore the child you named Jesus. St. Joseph, patron of the universal Church, pray with us that we may imitate you in lifelong dedication to the interests of the Savior."
Glory Be

Prayer to St. Joseph
O blessed St. Joseph, tender-hearted father, faithful guardian of Jesus, chaste spouse of the Mother of God, I pray and beseech you to offer God the Father my praise to Him through His divine Son, who died on the cross and rose again to give us sinners new life. Through the holy name of Jesus, pray with us that we may obtain from the eternal Father the favor we ask *(mention your request here)*. We have been

unfaithful to the unfailing love of God the Father; beg of Jesus mercy for us. Amid the splendors of God's loving presence, do not forget the sorrows of those who suffer, those who pray, those who weep. By your prayers and those of your most holy Spouse, our Blessed Lady, may the love of Jesus answer our call of confident hope. Amen.

EIGHTH DAY
Patron of the Hidden and Interior Life

Opening Prayer to St. Joseph for Faith
O blessed St. Joseph, heir of all the patriarchs, obtain for me this beautiful and precious virtue. Give me lively faith, which is the foundation of holiness, that faith that triumphs over all the temptations of the world and conquers human respect; a faith that cannot be shaken and that seeks God alone. In imitation of you, make me live by faith and submit my mind and heart to God, so that one day I may behold in heaven what I now firmly believe on earth.

Reading: Colossians 3:1-4 *(New Revised Standard Version)*
So if you have been raised with Christ, seek the things that are above, where Christ is, seated at the right hand of God. Set your minds on the things above, not on the things that are on earth, for you have died, and your life is hidden in Christ in God. When Christ who is your life is revealed, then you also will be revealed with him in glory.

Decade of St. Joseph Rosary *(consisting of the following)*

Our Father

Repeat the following prayer ten times: "Joseph, son of David, and husband of Mary; we honor you, guardian of the Redeemer, and we adore the child you named Jesus. St. Joseph, patron of the universal Church, pray with us that we may imitate you in lifelong dedication to the interests of the Savior."

Glory Be

Prayer to St. Joseph

O blessed St. Joseph, tender-hearted father, faithful guardian of Jesus, chaste spouse of the Mother of God, I pray and beseech you to offer God the Father my praise to Him through His divine Son, who died on the cross and rose again to give us sinners new life. Through the holy name of Jesus, pray with us that we may obtain from the eternal Father the favor we ask *(mention your request here)*. We have been unfaithful to the unfailing love of God the Father; beg of Jesus mercy for us. Amid the splendors of God's loving presence, do not forget the sorrows of those who suffer, those who pray, those who weep. By your prayers and those of your most holy Spouse, our Blessed Lady, may the love of Jesus answer our call of confident hope. Amen.

NINTH DAY
Patron and Model of the Church

Opening Prayer to St. Joseph for Faith

O blessed St. Joseph, heir of all the patriarchs, obtain for me this beautiful and precious virtue. Give me lively

faith, which is the foundation of holiness, that faith that triumphs over all the temptations of the world and conquers human respect; a faith that cannot be shaken and that seeks God alone. In imitation of you, make me live by faith and submit my mind and heart to God, so that one day I may behold in heaven what I now firmly believe on earth.

Reading: 1 Corinthians 12:12, 27 *(New Revised Standard Version)*

For just as the body is one and has many members, and all the members of the body though many, are one body, so it is with Christ. . . . Now you are the body of Christ and individually members of it.

Decade of St. Joseph Rosary *(consisting of the following)*

Our Father

Repeat the following prayer ten times: "Joseph, son of David, and husband of Mary; we honor you, guardian of the Redeemer, and we adore the child you named Jesus. St. Joseph, patron of the universal Church, pray with us that we may imitate you in lifelong dedication to the interests of the Savior."

Glory Be

Prayer to St. Joseph

O blessed St. Joseph, tender-hearted father, faithful guardian of Jesus, chaste spouse of the Mother of God, I pray and beseech you to offer God the Father my praise to Him through His divine Son, who died on the cross and rose again to give us sinners new life. Through the holy name of Jesus, pray with us that we may obtain from the eternal Father the favor we ask *(mention your request here)*. We have been unfaithful to the unfailing love of God the Father; beg of Jesus mercy for us. Amid the splendors of God's loving presence, do not forget the sorrows of those who suffer, those who pray, those who weep. By your prayers and those of your most holy Spouse, our Blessed Lady, may the love of Jesus answer our call of confident hope. Amen.

Shrine of St. Joseph, Guardian of the Redeemer

In answer to a solemn novena made by the Oblates of St. Joseph that God would provide a place for the building of a new seminary and church, a benefactor donated a tract of land on December 8, 1949. In two years the chapel and seminary had been built, but the Oblates' dream to build a shrine to St. Joseph would take another forty years.

In late 1991, a renovation project began that was completed in 1993. The chapel was solemnly dedicated in November of that year as the Shrine of St. Joseph, Guardian of the Redeemer. Pope John Paul's Apostolic Exhortation *Redemptoris Custos* (or "Guardian of the Redeemer") inspired the naming of the shrine.

The shrine is a center of devotion to St. Joseph for pilgrims near and far. It is a place of healing and reconciliation. It includes a St. Joseph Art Exhibit, a bookstore specializing in literature on St. Joseph as well as religious articles in his honor, and a publications center that produces a quarterly magazine, *Guardian of the Redeemer*.

Shrine of St. Joseph, Guardian of the Redeemer
Oblates of St. Joseph
544 West Cliff Drive
Santa Cruz, CA 95060
Telephone: 831-471-0442

CHAPTER 15
St. Jude

Patron of Hopeless Cases

History of the Devotion

Jude and Thaddeus are names that appear in the different lists of the Apostles in different Gospels. Most scholars seem to agree that they are the name of the same Apostle, Jude. Perhaps Luke's list (containing Thaddeus) already reflects an attempt not to confuse the name of Judas Iscariot with the other Judas who did not betray the Lord.

Jude Thaddeus speaks but once in the Gospels, in the Gospel of John where he says at the Last Supper to Jesus, "Lord, why do you intend to show yourself to us and not to the world?" (John 14:22; *New International Version*). It would seem to be a question that Jesus did not answer but merely reminded the Apostle that those who do the will of God will enjoy a special relationship with him.

There is some disagreement today as to whether the Apostle wrote the Letter of Jude, but there is a long history of belief that he did. In the letter he is identified with James, the first bishop of Jerusalem, and identified as a relative of Jesus. It is on this basis that in the devotional prayers St. Jude is referred to as such.

Jude is connected with the alleged early history of the Shroud of Turin. The king of Edessa (located in southern Turkey), Abagar, who suffered from leprosy, heard about the healing ministry of Jesus and wrote a letter asking the Lord to come to him. St. Jude arrived bearing a cloth that contained an imprint of the Lord's features. King Abagar, upon viewing the relic, was healed of his leprosy and converted. St. Jude is often portrayed as wearing the medallion bearing the image of Jesus commemorating this event.

Jude is often associated with Simon the Zealot, and early accounts have them venturing out together to spread the Gospel throughout modern-day Turkey, Iraq, and Iran. The two enjoyed great success in winning over converts to the Gospel but at a price.

The story is told that a Persian general consulted his magicians before deciding whether or not he should wage war with India. The magicians told the general that the war would be long and cause much suffering. The general then consulted the holy Apostles, who told him that India would quickly sue for peace if the general went to war with them. When he declared war on India, everything happened as the Apostles had predicted. The general ordered that the magicians be put to death.

The Apostles intervened on their behalf and the general relented. Soon after, as Jude and Simon were leaving the area, the magicians ambushed them, St. Jude being hacked to death with a hatchet.

Devotion to Jude has been recorded throughout the history of the Church. St. Bernard requested that a relic of St. Jude be buried with him. In her revelations of Jesus, St. Brigid of Sweden records Jesus as recommending that she turn to St. Jude as an intercessor. Devotion to St. Jude as the patron of hopeless cases can only be dated back to the mid-nineteenth century, and even then its origins are obscure like the saint himself. The spread of the devotion is a testament to the effectiveness of the prayer to St. Jude.

Novena to St. Jude

(The following prayers are repeated once a day for nine consecutive days.)

Most holy Apostle St. Jude, faithful servant and friend of Jesus, the name of the traitor who delivered your beloved Master into the hands of His enemies has caused you to be forgotten by many, but the Church honors and invokes you universally as the patron of hopeless cases, of things almost despaired of. Pray for me, I am so helpless and alone. Make use, I implore you, of that particular privilege given to you, to bring visible and speedy help where help is almost despaired of. Come to my assistance in this great need, that I may receive the consolation and help of heaven in all my necessities, tribulations, and sufferings, particularly *(mention your request here)* and that I may praise God with you and all the elect forever.

I promise, O blessed St. Jude, to be ever mindful of this great favor, to always honor you as my special and powerful patron, and to gratefully encourage devotion to you. Amen.

Our Father; Hail Mary; Glory Be

St. Jude Thaddeus, pray for us, and for all who invoke your aid.

National Shrine of St. Jude

The National Shrine of St. Jude has it origins in a pastor who, trying to build a church, was overwhelmed with the poverty of his parishioners. Claretian Father James Tort, the pastor of Our Lady of Guadalupe Church in 1929, had a strong devotion to St. Jude. He promised the saint that, in return for the saint's intercession in helping him find the money for the project, he would erect a shrine in St. Jude's honor. The church was built and the shrine erected.

The National Shrine of St. Jude
3200 East 91st Street
Chicago, IL 60617
Telephone: 312-236-7782
Website: http://www.stjudeleague.org

St. Jude Shrine

Another popular shrine to St. Jude in the United States is the St. Jude Shrine in Baltimore. Devotion to St. Jude began at the church in 1941. The services took on a sense of urgency with the involvement of the United States in World War II and continued ever afterward. The Pallottine Fathers and Brothers staff the shrine.

St. Jude Shrine
512 West Saratoga Street
Baltimore, MD 21201
Telephone: 410-685-6026
Website: http://www.stjudeshrine.org

Part 5

Novenas to Particular Saints

"[The saints'] intercession is their most exalted service to God's plan. We can and should ask them to intercede for us and for the whole world."

CATECHISM OF THE CATHOLIC CHURCH, NO. 2683

CHAPTER 16
St. Anthony of Padua

Miracle Worker

History of the Devotion

Ferdinand Bouillon was born in 1195 in Lisbon, Portugal. His parents, members of the Portuguese nobility, sent their son to the cathedral school. At the age of fifteen, Ferdinand entered the Canons Regular of St. Augustine. But after two years of being constantly distracted by the visits of his family, he moved to the Augustinian priory at Coimbra, which at the time was the capital of Portugal. During the next eight years, he immersed himself in studying the Scriptures and the early Fathers of the Church.

In 1220, the relics of Franciscans recently martyred in Morocco in the same year were brought to a church in Coimbra. After visiting the church and reverencing the holy remains, Ferdinand found that he was filled with an ardent longing to lay down his life for the sake of the Gospel. He wished to imitate the Franciscan martyrs in every way.

Ferdinand went to a Franciscan community near Coimbra and joined the community, taking the name Anthony after the great Egyptian desert Father. He made known his desire to go to Morocco and to preach the Gospel to the Saracens. His superiors permitted this, sending him to Morocco after he had been a Franciscan for a short time. But martyrdom was not to be his lot.

Anthony was stricken with illness from the time he arrived in Morocco in the fall; and when the illness still had not left him in the spring, he returned to Portugal. The ship never arrived at its destination because of a violent storm that blew the vessel off course, forcing the ship to drop anchor in Sicily. Here Anthony remained until he recovered from the illness and then set out for Assisi, where the Franciscans were holding a general chapter.

A short while after the general chapter, Anthony was called on to preach at an ordination. It was then that his remarkable gift for preaching was revealed. Word of the eloquence of Anthony soon reached St. Francis, who ordered Anthony to teach his fellow Franciscan brothers theology. His preaching opened the Scriptures to his listeners, winning over the lukewarm as well as heretics. He did not limit his gift to people but is said to have preached to the appreciative school of fish in the Brenta River.

Among his many miracles was an incident of bilocation. While he was preaching in a church, he remembered that he had forgotten to pray part of the Divine Office, something that he was under vows to do. As he continued to preach, he also suddenly appeared in the choir of brothers praying the office. Numerous other accounts of St. Anthony being in two places at the same time are also told.

There was no need for an umbrella with Anthony around. There are many stories of people listening to him preach being protected from rain that fell all around them but did not touch them.

It is said that Anthony radiated holiness, that sometimes his mere appearance led sinners to drop to their knees, repenting of their sins and seeking forgiveness. His life and ministry as a Franciscan lasted for eleven years when, in 1231, he fell ill and died at the age of thirty-six. He was canonized a year later by Pope Gregory IX. When his relics were being transferred in 1263, his body was found to have completely decomposed except his tongue, which was still lifelike and red in color. St. Bonaventure, present at the opening of the tomb, picked the tongue up from the coffin and kissed it, giving thanks for the gift that St. Anthony had possessed, that even in death his incorrupt tongue gave witness to God's gift.

St. Anthony's patronage for finding lost items and the intonation "Tony, Tony, please come 'round; something's lost and must be found" can be traced back to an event in Anthony's life when he found that his Breviary was missing. Not only did this Breviary contain the prayers he was bound to recite as priest but it also contained notes that he used both in his preaching and teaching. Anthony prayed that he would find it. A disgruntled friar who had left the order had stolen it but was moved to return not only the Breviary to Anthony but also himself to the order.

St. Anthony is often depicted as holding an open copy of the Scriptures and the Child Jesus standing on the text. The image speaks of how St. Anthony made Christ visible to those he preached to as he opened the meaning of the Scriptures to them. The image also makes reference to the countless visions of the Christ Child the saint is said to have experienced during his short life.

Novena to St. Anthony of Padua

(The following prayers are repeated once a day for nine consecutive days.)

Prayer to St. Anthony

O wonderful St. Anthony, glorious on account of the fame of your miracles, you had the happiness of receiving our Lord in your arms, in the form of a child. Obtain for me from His bounty the favor I ardently desire from the depths of my heart *(mention your request here)*. You who were so compassionate toward miserable sinners, regard not the demerits of the one who is praying to you, but God's glory to be again promoted by you, and the salvation of my soul, bound up with the requests I now so earnestly make. The pledge of my gratitude to you be the promise of a life in keeping with the Gospel teachings and devoted to the relief of the poor, who you loved so much. Bless my promise, and help me be faithful to it until death. Amen.

Prayer of Confidence to St. Anthony

Most holy St. Anthony, Beloved Friend of Jesus, I place myself in your heavenly care. Be with me, especially in life's troubles and difficulties. Intercede before the Lord for me, so that I may confidently know I do not face my problems alone. I join my prayers to yours, O Great Saint, as I ask God to give me consolation in times of sorrow, courage when I am afraid, and healing from all the ills that afflict me. Obtain for me from God, Most High, the grace to accept whatever is God's holy will for me and my loved ones. Strengthen my faith so that I will never despair, but always have hope in God's healing presence and power in my life. Amen.

National Shrine of St. Anthony

On a hillside overlooking Cincinnati is the estate donated to the Franciscans by Mr. and Mrs. A. Joseph Nurre in 1888. On the site the Franciscans built a chapel and friary. The chapel was dedicated to St. Anthony of Padua with the intention of it serving the friars who lived there.

People in the neighborhood began to make visits to the chapel, calling it St. Anthony's Shrine. In 1929, a small group who frequently came to pray at the shrine formed a group to promote devotion to the saint throughout the United States and to take care of the shrine. The small chapel offers an excellent place to pray and meditate on the saving and miraculous power of God.

St. Anthony Friary and Shrine
5000 Colerain Avenue
Cincinnati, OH 45223-1298
Telephone: 513-541-2146

CHAPTER 17

St. Gerard Majella

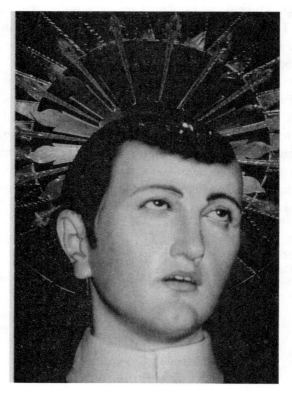

Patron of Expectant Mothers

History of the Devotion

Gerard Majella was born in Muro, Italy, in 1726, the son of Benedetta and Domenico, a tailor. When he was twelve, Gerard's father died and he was sent away as an apprentice to a tailor in a nearby town. When he had finished his apprenticeship, he was hired as a houseboy at the local bishop's residence. He remained in this task for a few years until the bishop died and then returned to his family's home with his mother and three sisters. Here he worked diligently, giving a third of all his earnings to his mother, another third to the poor, and the final third he handed over for the purpose of having Masses said for the poor souls in purgatory.

Gerard was said to have spent all of his spare time in church. He wanted to be a religious and twice applied to the Capuchins only to be turned down both times because of his frail nature.

Once, while attending a mission preached by the Redemptorists, he was so moved by their preaching that he sought to join their order. The Redemptorists were reluctant to take him into their community due to his appearance of poor health. Finally, however, he was able to convince them to allow him the role in their community as a humble brother.

Gerard soon became noted for his miracles. There is a story that once he traveled over a half-mile in the air. Many tales are told of his ability to bilocate. But perhaps his most impressive trait was his strong humility.

Neria Caggiano, a young woman he knew, went to the head of the Redemptorists, St. Alphonsus Liguori, with a tale that Gerard had not been chaste in his friendship with a woman that she had seen him with on occasion. Confronted with this accusation, Gerard did not deny it. Alphonsus did not want to believe it but nonetheless ordered that Gerard was not to receive Communion nor was he allowed to leave the community house.

Three months passed before Neria came to Alphonsus and confessed that she had made the story up. When St. Alphonsus asked Gerard why he had not spoken up in his defense, Gerard claimed that the holy rule that they lived under forbade him to make excuses.

His reputation as a miracle worker soon spread and he was besieged day and night by those seeking favors from God. His sickly nature and the miracles he wrought speak of God's power that works best in weakness. Once when he was traveling through a town and heard that the men had cut down a tree that a whole gang of them could not recover from the forest, he bade them to follow him. Tying a rope around the large tree lying on the ground, he commanded the creature of God to follow him. He pulled the large piece of timber by himself — with God's help of course.

Another story relates how Gerard assured a woman who was near death after going through an extremely difficult delivery of her child that she and her child would be fine and that he would pray for both. A few days later, the mother and child were of sound health, just as Gerard had predicted.

As he lay dying on his deathbed, a woman came to him telling him that he had left his handkerchief behind. Gerard told her to keep it, that one day she would need it. Years later during a difficult childbirth, when it seemed that she would die, she remembered the words of Gerard and took the handkerchief and placed it on her forehead and immediately the child was born and her health restored.

Gerard died at the age of twenty-nine, of tuberculosis, on the day that he had foretold. His dying words were to tell his brothers that the Blessed Virgin was there in the room; as he rose to greet her he died. Pope Pius X canonized Gerard in 1904. St. Gerard is often invoked as the patron saint of mothers and of safe delivery of children at birth.

Novena to St. Gerard Majella

(Strive each day to practice the virtue indicated in the petition.)

FIRST DAY

St. Gerard, ever full of faith, obtain for me that, believing firmly all that the Church of God proposes to my belief, I may strive to secure through a holy life the joys of eternal happiness. I pray that you also will pray for the special intention I bring to you of *(mention your request here).*

Hail Mary *(nine times along with the following)*
Pray for us, O St. Gerard, that we may be made worthy of the promises of Christ.

Let us pray:
O Almighty and Everlasting God, who did draw St. Gerard to Yourself, even from his childhood, making him conformable to the Image of Your Crucified Son, grant we beseech You, that imitating his example, we may be made like unto the same Divine Image, through Jesus Christ Our Lord. Amen.

SECOND DAY

St. Gerard, most generous saint, who from your youth did care so little for the goods of earth, grant that I may place all my confidence in Jesus Christ alone, my true Treasure, who alone can make me happy in time and eternity. I pray that you also will pray for the special intention I bring to you of *(mention your request here)*.

Hail Mary *(nine times along with the following)*
Pray for us, O St. Gerard, that we may be made worthy of the promises of Christ.

Let us pray:
O Almighty and Everlasting God, who did draw St. Gerard to Yourself, even from his childhood, making him conformable to the Image of Your Crucified Son, grant we beseech You, that imitating his example, we may be made like unto the same Divine Image, through Jesus Christ Our Lord. Amen.

THIRD DAY

St. Gerard, bright seraph of love, who, despising all earthly love, did consecrate your life to the service of God and your neighbor, promoting God's glory in your lowly state, and ever ready to assist the distressed and console the sorrowful, obtain for me, I beseech you, that, loving God the only Good and my neighbor for His sake, I may be hereafter united to Him forever in glory. I pray that you also will pray for the special intention I bring to you of *(mention your request here)*.

Hail Mary *(nine times along with the following)*
Pray for us, O St. Gerard, that we may be made worthy of the promises of Christ.

Let us pray:

O Almighty and Everlasting God, who did draw St. Gerard to Yourself, even from his childhood, making him conformable to the Image of Your Crucified Son, grant we beseech You, that imitating his example, we may be made like unto the same Divine Image, through Jesus Christ Our Lord. Amen.

FOURTH DAY

St. Gerard, spotless lily of purity, by your angelic virtue and your wonderful innocence of life you did receive from the Infant Jesus and His Immaculate Mother, sweet pledges of tenderest love, grant, I beseech you, that I may ever strive courageously in my lifelong fight, and thus win the crown that awaits the brave and the true. I pray that you also will pray for the special intention I bring to you of *(mention your request here)*.

Hail Mary *(nine times along with the following)*
Pray for us, O St. Gerard, that we may be made worthy of the promises of Christ.

Let us pray:

O Almighty and Everlasting God, who did draw St. Gerard to Yourself, even from his childhood, making him conformable to the Image of Your Crucified Son, grant we beseech You, that imitating his example, we may be made like unto the same Divine Image, through Jesus Christ Our Lord. Amen.

FIFTH DAY

St. Gerard, model of holy obedience, who through your life did heroically submit your judgment to those who represent Jesus Christ to you, thus sanctifying your lowliest actions, obtain for me from God cheerful submission to His Holy Will and the virtue of perfect obedience, that I may be made conformable to Jesus, my Model, who was obedient even to death. I pray that you also will pray for the special intention I bring to you of *(mention your request here)*.

Hail Mary *(nine times along with the following)*
Pray for us, O St. Gerard, that we may be made worthy of the promises of Christ.

Let us pray:
O Almighty and Everlasting God, who did draw St. Gerard to Yourself, even from his childhood, making him conformable to the Image of Your Crucified Son, grant we beseech You, that imitating his example, we may be made like unto the same Divine Image, through Jesus Christ Our Lord. Amen.

SIXTH DAY

St. Gerard, most perfect imitator of Jesus Our Redeemer, you whose greatest glory was to be humble and lowly, obtain that I, too, knowing how little I am in God's sight, may be found worthy to enter the kingdom that is promised to the humble and lowly of heart. I pray that you also will pray for the special intention I bring to you of *(mention your request here)*.

Hail Mary *(nine times along with the following)*
Pray for us, O St. Gerard, that we may be made worthy of the promises of Christ.

Let us pray:
O Almighty and Everlasting God, who did draw St. Gerard to Yourself, even from his childhood, making him conformable to the Image of Your Crucified Son, grant we beseech You, that imitating his example, we may be made like unto the same Divine Image, through Jesus Christ Our Lord. Amen.

SEVENTH DAY
St. Gerard, unconquered hero, most patient in suffering, you who gloried in infirmity, and under slander and most cruel ignominy did rejoice to suffer with Christ, obtain for me patience and resignation in my sorrows, that I may bravely bear the cross that is to gain for me the crown of everlasting glory. I pray that you also will pray for the special intention I bring to you of *(mention your request here)*.

Hail Mary *(nine times along with the following)*
Pray for us, O St. Gerard, that we may be made worthy of the promises of Christ.

Let us pray:
O Almighty and Everlasting God, who did draw St. Gerard to Yourself, even from his childhood, making him conformable to the Image of Your Crucified Son, grant we beseech You, that imitating his example, we may be made

like unto the same Divine Image, through Jesus Christ Our Lord. Amen.

EIGHTH DAY

St. Gerard, true lover of Jesus in the Blessed Sacrament of the Altar, you who knelt long hours before the tabernacle, and there tasted the joys of paradise, obtain for me an undying love for the Most Holy Sacrament, that thus receiving frequently the Body and Blood of Jesus, I may daily grow in His holy love and merit the priceless grace of loving Him even to the end. I pray that you also will pray for the special intention I bring to you of *(mention your request here)*.

Hail Mary *(nine times along with the following)*
Pray for us, O St. Gerard, that we may be made worthy of the promises of Christ.

Let us pray:
O Almighty and Everlasting God, who did draw St. Gerard to Yourself, even from his childhood, making him conformable to the Image of Your Crucified Son, grant we beseech You, that imitating his example, we may be made like unto the same Divine Image, through Jesus Christ Our Lord. Amen.

NINTH DAY

St. Gerard, most favored child of heaven, to whom Mary gave the Infant Jesus in the days of your childhood, to whom she sweetly came before and did close your eyes in death, obtain for me I beseech you, so to seek and love my Blessed Mother during life, that she may be my joy and consolation in this valley of tears, until with you, before the throne of God, I may praise her goodness for all eternity. I pray that you also will pray for the special intention I bring to you of *(mention your request here)*.

Hail Mary *(nine times along with the following)*
Pray for us, O St. Gerard, that we may be made worthy of the promises of Christ.

Let us pray:
O Almighty and Everlasting God, who did draw St. Gerard to Yourself, even from his childhood, making him conformable to the Image of Your Crucified Son, grant we beseech You, that imitating his example, we may be made like unto the same Divine Image, through Jesus Christ Our Lord. Amen.

National Shrine of
St. Gerard Majella

Italian immigrants to St. Lucy's parish brought devotion to St. Gerard to the United States from Italy in 1899. They established the Shrine of St. Gerard in a side chapel in St. Lucy's Church, erecting a life-size statue of St. Gerard from Italy and enshrining a relic of his bones. The devotion attached to the chapel led to its being dedicated as a national shrine by the archbishop of Newark in1977.

Those seeking the intercession of St. Gerard visit the shrine throughout the year, and special celebrations are held annually around the saint's feast day, October 16.

National Shrine of St. Gerard Majella
St. Lucy's Church
118 Seventh Avenue
Newark, NJ 07104
Telephone: 973-482-6663

CHAPTER 18

St. Peregrine

The Cancer Saint

History of the Devotion

Peregrine Laziosi's early life was anything but saintly. He was noted for being deeply involved in violent political activities as a youth growing up in the city of Forlì, Italy. Ironically, it was during one of his unruly activities that he was converted.

It happened that a saintly friar was preaching in Forlì and was attempting to convince the citizens to make peace with the pope, who had placed the city under interdict. Joining other ruffians, Peregrine decided to make sport of the man who would later be known as St. Philip Benizi, of the Order of Servants of Mary (Servites). At first he merely heckled Philip as he tried to preach, but eventually he leaped upon the priest and attacked him, landing a vicious blow to the cheek of St. Philip. Philip's response was to offer Peregrine the other cheek.

This bothered Peregrine, and he returned the following day to find Philip and to apologize. Like Saul who was converted in the midst of persecuting the Church, Peregrine eventually joined St. Philip and the Servites as a choir-brother. Over the years he was revered for his great sanctity.

Another event that happened to him later in life has made St. Peregrine a saint for modern times. Peregrine was diagnosed with cancer of the bone in his leg. The doctors had determined that the only cure for this ailment was to amputate the diseased member. Late on the eve of the operation, Peregrine dragged himself into the chapter room to pray. During his prayer before a crucifix, he envisioned the hand of Jesus detach itself from the cross and touch his cancerous leg. The healing was immediate, to the amazement of both Peregrine and the doctor.

People who have the sad misfortune of being diagnosed with cancer find hope in prayer to St. Peregrine. His life shows the power of Christ to touch not only the cancers that can afflict our bodies but also the cancer of sin that can destroy our souls. As Jesus said, "Do not be afraid of those who can kill the body but cannot kill the soul. Rather, be afraid of the One who can destroy both soul and body in hell" (Matthew 10:28).

Novena to St. Peregrine

FIRST DAY
Prayer for Sincere Repentance

O glorious St. Peregrine, true model of conversion to God, where once you gave yourself to God, you generously entered the religious Order of Servants of Mary and henceforth led a life of heroic penance.

Obtain for me, I beseech you, the grace to never return to my sins, to do penance for them, and from now on, to lead a holy and fervent life. May I also, after your example, love our Blessed Crucified Lord, and bear patiently all the trials, sufferings, and infirmities that may be my lot in life. I ask this through Christ our Lord. Amen.

Prayer to St. Peregrine

O great St. Peregrine, you have been called "The Mighty" and "The Wonder Worker" because of the numerous miracles which you have obtained from God for those who have had recourse to you. You who for so many years bore in your own flesh the dread disease of cancer, and when human power could do no more, you had recourse to Jesus crucified. He answered you by coming down from the cross and healing your affliction. Ask of God and Our Lady the cure of these sick persons whom we entrust to you *(mention your request here)*.

Aided in this way by your powerful intercession, we shall sing to God, now and for all eternity, a song of gratitude for His great goodness and mercy. Amen.

Our Father; Hail Mary
St. Peregrine, pray for us.

SECOND DAY
Prayer for Perseverance

St. Peregrine, you have left us an example to follow. As a penitent, you were humble enough to acknowledge your sin before God and man. As a Servite religious you were faithful in fulfilling your commitments. As an invalid, you were patient in bearing your illness. Intercede for us to our Father through Christ, so that we may be humble, steadfast, and patient, and that He may grant the favors we ask. Amen.

Prayer to St. Peregrine

O great St. Peregrine, you have been called "The Mighty" and "The Wonder Worker" because of the numerous miracles which you have obtained from God for those who have had recourse to you. You who for so many years bore in your own flesh the dread disease of cancer, and when human power could do no more, you had recourse to Jesus crucified. He answered you by coming down from the cross and healing your affliction. Ask of God and Our Lady the cure of these sick persons whom we entrust to you *(mention your request here)*.

Aided in this way by your powerful intercession, we shall sing to God, now and for all eternity, a song of gratitude for His great goodness and mercy. Amen.

Our Father; Hail Mary
St. Peregrine, pray for us.

THIRD DAY
Prayer for Humility

O most holy and humble Peregrine, great indeed were your merits, yet you always fulfilled the lowliest office toward your brother Servites, nor would you aspire to be ordained to the priesthood, except under obedience at the express command of your superiors. Obtain for me true humility of heart, so that my life may be hid with Christ in God and be made worthy of His grace and favor. Amen.

Prayer to St. Peregrine

O great St. Peregrine, you have been called "The Mighty" and "The Wonder Worker" because of the numerous miracles which you have obtained from God for those who have had recourse to you. You who for so many years bore in your own flesh the dread disease of cancer, and when human power could do no more, you had recourse to Jesus crucified. He answered you by coming down from the cross and healing your affliction. Ask of God and Our Lady the cure of these sick persons whom we entrust to you *(mention your request here)*.

Aided in this way by your powerful intercession, we shall sing to God, now and for all eternity, a song of gratitude for His great goodness and mercy. Amen.

Our Father; Hail Mary
St. Peregrine, pray for us.

FOURTH DAY
Prayer for Patience

O St. Peregrine, unconquered in patience, you not only accepted the customary trials and disappointments of life which we are all subject to, you also endured in silence the acute pain of an incurable sore. How lovingly did our Crucified Savior reward your faith and long suffering, when by a miracle unheard of before, He healed your cruel sore, touching it with His divine hand! Obtain for me, I beseech you, that I, too, may practice patience and mortification and thus expiate my sins, and some day share in those consolations that you enjoy in heaven. Amen.

Prayer to St. Peregrine

O great St. Peregrine, you have been called "The Mighty" and "The Wonder Worker" because of the numerous miracles which you have obtained from God for those who have had recourse to you. You who for so many years bore in your own flesh the dread disease of cancer, and when human power could do no more, you had recourse to Jesus crucified. He answered you by coming down from the cross and healing your affliction. Ask of God and Our Lady the cure of these sick persons whom we entrust to you *(mention your request here)*.

Aided in this way by your powerful intercession, we shall sing to God, now and for all eternity, a song of gratitude for His great goodness and mercy. Amen.

Our Father; Hail Mary
St. Peregrine, pray for us.

FIFTH DAY
Prayer for Zeal for Souls

O holy apostle St. Peregrine, full of zeal for the conversion of sinners, and never wearied in preaching the divine word, you brought sinners back to penance and promoted the honor and glory of God in all the land. Obtain, I beseech you, that I may not be content with working but my salvation alone, but may also seek to sanctify my neighbor by good example, continued prayer, and kindly counsel. How happy I would be if l could thus promote the glory of God on earth and have my part with you and all the saints in the eternal glory of heaven. Amen.

Prayer to St. Peregrine

O great St. Peregrine, you have been called "The Mighty" and "The Wonder Worker" because of the numerous miracles which you have obtained from God for those who have had recourse to you. You who for so many years bore in your own flesh the dread disease of cancer, and when human power could do no more, you had recourse to Jesus crucified. He answered you by coming down from the cross and healing your affliction. Ask of God and Our Lady the cure of these sick persons whom we entrust to you *(mention your request here)*.

Aided in this way by your powerful intercession, we shall sing to God, now and for all eternity, a song of gratitude for His great goodness and mercy. Amen.

Our Father; Hail Mary
St. Peregrine, pray for us.

SIXTH DAY
Prayer for Sinners

Lord, I know there exists another cancer: that of the soul. I beg you to save all sinners from this disease through the merits and intercession of your faithful servant, St. Peregrine. I know that cancer is an unnatural growth in the body and in the same way moral cancer is an unnatural growth in our souls that destroys our true life. Do not permit your grace to be destroyed in me by this cancerous growth, and grant forgiveness to those poor souls who are victims of this dreadful cancer of the soul. Grant this through the intercession of your humble servant, St. Peregrine. Amen.

Prayer to St. Peregrine

O great St. Peregrine, you have been called "The Mighty" and "The Wonder Worker" because of the numerous miracles which you have obtained from God for those who have had recourse to you. You who for so many years bore in your own flesh the dread disease of cancer, and when human power could do no more, you had recourse to Jesus crucified. He answered you by coming down from the cross and healing your affliction. Ask of God and Our Lady the cure of these sick persons whom we entrust to you *(mention your request here)*.

Aided in this way by your powerful intercession, we shall sing to God, now and for all eternity, a song of gratitude for His great goodness and mercy. Amen.

Our Father; Hail Mary
St. Peregrine, pray for us.

SEVENTH DAY
Prayer for Peace

O glorious St. Peregrine, by your conversion at the feet of St. Philip, you succeeded in bringing peace to your native land. Obtain peace for us in this vale of tears and strife — peace for families, peace for country, peace among nations. May I, in my own life, promote this peace by reconciling myself to those who have injured me, or whom I may have injured. May I forgive others as I wish to be forgiven by God. Obtain this favor for me, dear St. Peregrine. Amen.

Prayer to St. Peregrine

O great St. Peregrine, you have been called "The Mighty" and "The Wonder Worker" because of the numerous miracles which you have obtained from God for those who have had recourse to you. You who for so many years bore in your own flesh the dread disease of cancer, and when human power could do no more, you had recourse to Jesus crucified. He answered you by coming down from the cross and healing your affliction. Ask of God and Our Lady the cure of these sick persons whom we entrust to you *(mention your request here)*.

Aided in this way by your powerful intercession, we shall sing to God, now and for all eternity, a song of gratitude for His great goodness and mercy. Amen.

Our Father; Hail Mary
St. Peregrine, pray for us.

EIGHTH DAY
Prayer for Resignation

O dear St. Peregrine, I turn to you in my hour of suffering and need. Obtain for me the wisdom and strength to see God's loving design in all the workings of His providence. St. Peregrine, repentant sinner, devoted religious, saint upon earth, and crowned saint in heaven, secure for me the graces that are best for me, and the outcome of my illness which is in complete accord with the blessed providence of God. Amen.

Prayer to St. Peregrine

O great St. Peregrine, you have been called "The Mighty" and "The Wonder Worker" because of the numerous miracles which you have obtained from God for those who have had recourse to you. You who for so many years bore in your own flesh the dread disease of cancer, and when human power could do no more, you had recourse to Jesus crucified. He answered you by coming down from the cross and healing your affliction. Ask of God and Our Lady the cure of these sick persons whom we entrust to you *(mention your request here)*.

Aided in this way by your powerful intercession, we shall sing to God, now and for all eternity, a song of gratitude for His great goodness and mercy. Amen.

Our Father; Hail Mary
St. Peregrine, pray for us.

NINTH DAY
Prayer for Final Perseverance

Lord, I know that I must die someday, and that sickness is but a preparation for death, for that liberation which will free us from all the miseries of this life and will lead us to eternal life, which we hope to share with the blessed in heaven. Grant me the gift of perseverance to the end, so that when my summons comes, it may find me in the state of your friendship. St. Peregrine, assist me at the hour of death. Intercede for me to the Divine Heart of Jesus and to the Sorrowful Mother whom you served so well in your life. I ask this through Christ our Lord. Amen.

Prayer to St. Peregrine

O great St. Peregrine, you have been called "The Mighty" and "The Wonder Worker" because of the numerous miracles which you have obtained from God for those who have had recourse to you. You who for so many years bore in your own flesh the dread disease of cancer, and when human power could do no more, you had recourse to Jesus crucified. He answered you by coming down from the cross and healing your affliction. Ask of God and Our Lady the cure of these sick persons whom we entrust to you *(mention your request here)*.

Aided in this way by your powerful intercession, we shall sing to God, now and for all eternity, a song of gratitude for His great goodness and mercy. Amen.

Our Father; Hail Mary
St. Peregrine, pray for us.

St. Peregrine Center at The Grotto

The Grotto began as the dream of Father Ambrose Mayer, a Servite friar who as a child had promised God to do something great for the Church if his prayer for his mother's health would be heard. His mother survived, and Ambrose did not forget his promise; years later, he purchased land in Oregon and, in 1924, established the Sanctuary of Our Sorrowful Mother.

The St. Peregrine Center at The Grotto was founded in 1974. Devotion to the saint is celebrated monthly with Mass, sacramental Anointing of the Sick, and blessing with the relic of St. Peregrine. Prayer intentions may be left on The Grotto's website and will be remembered in the monthly celebration of Mass.

The Grotto
The National Sanctuary of Our Sorrowful Mother
NE 85th and Sandy Boulevard
P.O. Box 20008
Portland, OR 97294-0008
Telephone: 503-254-7371
Fax: 503-254-7948
E-mail: grottog2@teleport.com
Website: http://www.thegrotto.org

CHAPTER 19
St. Rita of Cascia

Saint of the Impossible

History of the Devotion

Rita Lotti was born near Cascia in Italy in the fourteenth century, the only child of her parents, Antonio and Amata. Her parents were official peacemakers in a turbulent environment of feuding families.

At an early age Rita felt called to religious life; however, her parents arranged for her to be married to Paolo Mancini. Rita accepted this as God's will for her, and the newlyweds were soon blessed with two sons.

One day while on his way home, Paolo was killed. Rita's grief was compounded with the fear that her two sons would seek to avenge their father's death, as was the custom of the time. She began praying and fasting that God would not allow this to happen. Both sons soon fell ill and died, which Rita saw as an answer to her prayers.

Now alone in the world, Rita sought to enter religious life, feeling that God had cleared the path for her to fulfill the vocation that she had felt was hers from childhood. Yet she found that the convent she so desired to enter was reluctant to accept her due to fears that the political rivals that had killed her husband would bring violence on them.

She finally brought peace between the rivals and was able to enter the Convent of St. Mary Magdalene of the Augustinian Nuns. In religious life, Rita was noted for her holiness. She spent her days not only in prayer and contemplation but also in service to the sick and the poor.

One day while kneeling in prayer and contemplating the passion of Jesus, she received the wound of one thorn from the crown of thorns that she bore until her death some fifteen years later.

Devotion to St. Rita was almost nonexistent for five hundred years, but with her canonization in 1900, all of that has changed. She is truly a saint for every state in life, having spent her life as a married woman, a mother, a widow, and a religious.

Novena to St. Rita of Cascia

(The following prayers are repeated once a day for nine consecutive days.)

Prayer to the Holy Spirit *(see "Prayers Common to Novenas," p. 252)*

Litany of St. Rita of Cascia

Lord, have mercy on us. Christ, have mercy on us.
Christ, hear us. Christ, graciously hear us.
God, the Father of heaven, have mercy on us.
God, the Son, Redeemer of the world, have mercy on us.
God, the Holy Spirit, have mercy on us.
Holy Trinity, one God, have mercy on us.
Immaculate Mary, Mother of God, pray for us.
Holy Mary, Mother of pure love, pray for us.
Holy Mary, Comforter of the afflicted, pray for us.
Holy Mary, Queen of all the saints, pray for us.
Holy Mary, Model of life for St. Rita, pray for us.
St. Rita, our advocate and protectress, pray for us.
St. Rita, beloved of the Lord, pray for us.
St. Rita, given special grace from heaven, pray for us.
St. Rita, remarkable in childhood, pray for us.
St. Rita, model of obedience to God's will, pray for us.
St. Rita, of untiring patience, pray for us.
St. Rita, model of Christian mothers, pray for us.
St. Rita, mirror for Christian spouses, pray for us.
St. Rita, heroic in sacrifice, pray for us.
St. Rita, generous in forgiving, pray for us.
St. Rita, martyr in penitence, pray for us.
St. Rita, embracing humility and poverty, pray for us.

St. Rita, exemplary as a widow, pray for us.

St. Rita, prompt to answer the divine call, pray for us.

St. Rita, patient in suffering, pray for us.

St. Rita, mirror of religious observance, pray for us.

St. Rita, mystical rose of every virtue, pray for us.

St. Rita, enamored of the Passion of Christ, pray for us.

St. Rita, pierced with a thorn, pray for us.

St. Rita, in ecstasy before the Blessed Sacrament, pray for us.

St. Rita, consumed with Divine Love, pray for us.

St. Rita, received into heaven with joy, pray for us.

St. Rita, incorrupt in your chaste body, pray for us.

St. Rita, advocate of impossible cases, pray for us.

St. Rita, persevering in prayer, pray for us.

St. Rita, help of those in need, pray for us.

Lamb of God, who takes away the sins of the world, spare us, O Lord.

Lamb of God, who takes away the sins of the world, graciously hear us, O Lord.

Lamb of God, who takes away the sins of the world, have mercy on us.

Lord, You have signed Your servant Rita with the marks of Your love and Passion.

Let us pray:

O God, who bestowed on St. Rita such grace that she loved her enemies, and bore in her heart and on her forehead the mark of Your love and Passion, grant us, we beseech You, through her merits and intercession, a love for our enemies. Through our contemplation of Your sufferings and Passion, may we merit the reward promised to the meek and suffering. You live and reign forever. Amen.

Prayer of Petition

Glorious St. Rita, patroness of those in need, your intercession with the Lord is most powerful. Through the favors obtained by your prayers you have been called "Advocate of hopeless and even impossible cases." St. Rita, humble and pure, patient and compassionate lover of Christ Crucified! We have confidence that everyone who has recourse to you will find comfort and relief. Listen to our petitions and show your power with God on our behalf. Obtain our petitions for us if they are for the greater honor of God, and for our good. We promise, if our petitions are granted, to make known your favor and to glorify God for his gift. Relying on your power with the merciful Savior, we ask of you *(mention your request here).*

By the singular merits of your childhood, obtain our request for us.

By your perfect union with the Divine Will, obtain our request for us.

By your acceptance of troubles in your married life, obtain our request for us.

By the anguish felt at the murder of your husband, obtain our request for us.

By the surrender of your children rather than have them offend God, obtain our request for us.

By your miraculous entrance into the convent, obtain our request for us.

By your daily penance and fasting, obtain our request for us.

By your courage and joy in bearing the mark of the Crucified Savior, obtain our request for us.

By the Divine Love that consumed your life, obtain our request for us.

By your devotion in receiving the Blessed Sacrament, obtain our request for us.

By the happiness you felt in leaving this life for union with Christ, obtain our request for us.

By the example you have given to people of every state of life, obtain our request for us.

Pray for us, St. Rita, that we may be made worthy of the promises of Christ.

Let us pray:

Heavenly Father! In Your infinite love and mercy You heed the prayer of Your beloved servant Rita. You graciously grant favors, through her intercession, which are considered impossible to human skill and effort. Relying on her compassionate love we ask You to assist us in our trials and difficulties. Let unbelievers know that You are the helper of the humble, the defender of the weak, and the strength of those who trust in You. We ask this through Christ our Lord. Amen.

National Shrine of
St. Rita of Cascia

Seven years after the canonization of St. Rita, the Augustinian friars founded a parish in her honor in the city of Philadelphia. Devotion to St. Rita was very popular and, in 1915, the Church that served the large Italian immigrant population was completed. The friars established a novena to St. Rita that was prayed a number of times both on Sundays and Wednesdays to an overflowing church.

Today the novena to St. Rita is prayed solemnly at the St. Rita of Cascia Shrine for the nine days leading up to St. Rita's feast on May 22. It is also prayed three times every Wednesday along with veneration of a relic of St. Rita throughout the year. Prayer petitions may be left at the shrine website.

St. Rita of Cascia Shrine
1166 South Broad Street
Philadelphia, PA 19146
Telephone: 215-546-8333
E-mail: ritashrine@aol.com
Website: http://www.saintritashrine.org/

CHAPTER 20

St. Thérèse of Lisieux

"The Little Flower,"
Doctor of the Church

History of the Devotion

Marie Françoise Thérèse Martin was born on January 2, 1873, to Louis Martin, a watchmaker, and his wife, Zélie Marie Guérin, a maker of lace, in Alençon, France. Marie Francis was called by her middle name, Thérèse, because she had an older sister already named Marie. When Thérèse was four years old, her mother died and her father moved to Lisieux to be near his deceased wife's sister who he hoped would look after his five daughters.

The motherless Thérèse grew very attached to her sisters, who one by one left to join the Carmelites of Lisieux. First Pauline entered when Thérèse was nine; then her sister Marie followed when Thérèse was nearly fourteen. Shortly after this, Thérèse says that she had a conversion that occurred on Christmas Eve when it seemed to her that the Infant Jesus filled her soul with light.

Wishing to follow her two sisters into the Carmel, she made her wish known to her father in May of 1887, when she was about fourteen and a half years old. Louis Martin gave his assent to her request, but the nuns at the Carmel would not hear of it because of her young age. An appeal to the local bishop also met the same response. A short time after her attempted entrance into the Carmel of Lisieux, she went on pilgrimage with her father to Rome.

During an audience with Pope Leo XIII, it became time for Thérèse to approach the Holy Father to silently receive his blessing. She broke the silence and asked him in honor of his priestly jubilee to grant her request to enter the Carmelites. He did not grant her request but told her that she would enter the Carmelites when God willed it.

Soon after the father and daughter returned to Lisieux, the bishop changed his ruling and Thérèse entered the Carmelites at Lisieux at the age of fifteen on April 9, 1888. She was professed a little over two years later. Her years at the Carmel were spent in prayer and living out her vocation in simplicity. She took her vocation to pray for priests seriously and prayed especially for a priest who had left the Catholic Church and started a new church, an ex-Carmelite named

Hyacinthe Loyson. She also greatly desired to go to Hanoi and to be with the Carmelites there, but the sickness that plagued her short life grew worse before she could ever leave. On September 30, 1897, she died at the age of twenty-four.

Devotion to Thérèse spread very fast, and her story became well known through *The Story of a Soul*, the autobiography that she had written under the obedience of her sister, who was her Mother Superior at the Carmel of Lisieux. Her "Little Way" might be described as a way of living each day with the realization that we are all children of God.

Thérèse of Lisieux was canonized a saint by Pope Pius XI in 1925. St. Thérèse had prophesied that she would "make God loved" after her death and that she would spend her time in heaven doing good on earth, showering roses. It is a common belief among devotees of St. Thérèse that she often sends roses to those who seek her intercession. Sometimes they come in an unexpected card from someone, sometimes in actual roses.

St. Thérèse of the Child Jesus was declared a Doctor of the Church by Pope John Paul II in October of 1997 because of the profound impact she has had on the life of the Church over the last century.

Novena to St. Thérèse of Lisieux

(The following prayers are repeated once a day for nine consecutive days.)

Prayer to St. Thérèse

O glorious St. Thérèse, whom Almighty God raised up to aid and inspire the human family, I implore your miraculous intercession. You are so powerful in obtaining every need of body and spirit from the Heart of God. Holy Mother Church proclaims you a "Prodigy of Miracles . . . the Greatest Saint of Modern times." Now I fervently beseech you to answer my petition and to carry out your promises of spending heaven doing good upon earth . . . of letting fall from heaven a shower of roses. Little Flower, give me your childlike faith, to see the Face of God in the people and experiences of my life, and to love God with full confidence. St. Thérèse, my Carmelite Sister, I will fulfill your plea "to be made known everywhere" and I will continue to lead others to Jesus through you. Amen.

Novena Rose Prayer

O Little Thérèse of the Child Jesus, please pick for me a rose from the heavenly gardens and send it to me as a message of love.

O Little Flower of Jesus, ask God today to grant the favors I now place with confidence in your hands *(mention your request here)*.

St. Thérèse, help me to always believe, as you did, in God's great love for me so that I might imitate your "Little Way" each day. Amen.

National Shrine of St. Thérèse

The National Shrine of St. Thérèse was built in 1987 to replace the previous place of devotion that had existed in downtown Chicago at St. Clara's Church, which was destroyed by a fire in 1975. The shrine is located just outside of Chicago on beautiful grounds. A museum at the entrance of the chapel includes a painting of Thérèse done by her sister Céline. A map of North America drawn by Thérèse, her prayer book, and the chair she used to write her autobiography are also in the museum.

The chapel includes the largest religious wood carving in the United States. This impressive piece highlights the scenes of Thérèse's life. Beneath the carving is a reliquary containing first-class relics of Thérèse.

The shrine also has a unique collection of images of Our Lady of Mount Carmel from around the world.

National Shrine of St. Thérèse
8501 Bailey Road
Darien, IL 60561-0065
Telephone: 630-969-3311
E-mail: webmaster@littleflower.org
Website: http://www.saint-therese.org/

Part 6

Novenas to American Saints

"As you sent me into the world, I have sent them into the world. For them I sanctify myself, that they too may be truly sanctified."

JOHN 17:18-19

CHAPTER 21

North American Martyrs

Seed of Christianity in the United States and Canada

History of the Devotion

Eight men gave their lives for Christ in the New World, between the years of 1642 and 1649, each of them connected with the Jesuits who were attempting to learn the culture of the indigenous people and to preach the Gospel to them in a way that would be understood. Their martyrdom might be looked at by some as a failure, but the witness of an Algonquin-Mohawk maiden born seven years after the last of the Jesuits had been martyred would prove otherwise. Three of the martyrs were put to death in what today is Auriesville, New York. We will focus on those martyrs. The other five — Antoine Daniel, Jean de Brébeuf, Gabriel Lalemant, Charles Garnier, and Noël Chabanel — were all martyred near Midland, Ontario, in Canada.

René Goupil was the first to meet with martyrdom. He had studied for the Jesuits in his native France but only for a while before pursuing a career in medicine. When he heard that the Jesuits were sending a mission to North America, he volunteered his services. Shortly after his arrival in New France, René ended up with Father Isaac Jogues and a group of Hurons on their way to a Huron village up the river when a warring Mohawk tribe ambushed them. They suffered excruciating torture at the hands of the Mohawks, including running a gauntlet where they were beaten, having the hair both on their head and face torn out, fingernails ripped off, and their forefingers cut off both by having them chewed on and cut with a sharp clam shell. When the torture ended, Father Jogues and Goupil were made slaves. On September 29, 1642, René Goupil was tomahawked to death when he was seen to be making the Sign of the Cross over a Mohawk child. His body was thrown into a ravine.

Father Jogues remained a slave to a Mohawk family but escaped with the help of a Dutch Reformed minister in what today is Albany, New York. Soon he was able to travel to New Amsterdam, present-day New York City. Finally he made it back to France. Because of his deformities he had to gain a special dispensation from the pope so that he could resume saying the Mass. Pope Urban VIII granted him the dispensation, saying, "It is unbefitting that a martyr of Christ should not drink the blood of Christ." Father Jogues became the toast of France and was invited by the royalty to tell his tale of New France. This embarrassed him and he asked to be sent back to the missions. Already familiar with the language of the Mohawks, which he had learned during his imprisonment, he was chosen to represent the government of France in their dealings with the Mohawks.

In the late spring of 1646, he was sent back to the place of his previous torture to negotiate a peace treaty with the Mohawks. He returned from this journey in the early summer, and then made another journey, this time along with a companion, Jean Lalande. The tribe was not happy when these Frenchmen from France arrived whom they blamed for the recent crop failure and plague. On October 18, 1646, the tribe invited Father Jogues into their lodge. As he entered, they severed his head. They threw his body into the Mohawk River and impaled his head on a post at the entrance of their stockade. They did the same to Lalande the next day, placing his head next to that of Father Jogues.

Ten years after St. Isaac Jogues was martyred, Kateri Tekakwitha was born in the same village where the three martyrs had tried to plant Christianity. Kateri's mother was a captured Algonquin Christian who passed on the faith to her daughter even though her father, a Mohawk, was hostile to the faith. While she was still a child, an outbreak of smallpox took the life of both of her parents and brother, and left her disfigured for the rest of her life. When Jesuit missionaries visited the village that is near modern-day Fonda, New York, they baptized Kateri on Easter Sunday of 1676.

It was apparently at this time that she also consecrated herself to Christ, vowing perpetual virginity. Her foster parents wished her to marry; but in order to preserve her vow, she had to escape, with the help of one of the Jesuit priests, to a village of Christians in Canada. Here she received her First Communion and continued to advance in holiness. She suffered ridicule during her short life both for her faith and her facial disfigurement.

All of that ended on April 17, 1680, at the age of twenty-four, when she died. Her dying words were, "Jesus, I love you," which she repeated over and over. After her death, her face (which had been deeply scarred) appeared to be miraculously made whole.

In 1980, Pope John Paul II beatified Kateri. The novena to the North American Martyrs ends with a prayer for Kateri's canonization.

Novena to the North American Martyrs

(The following prayers are repeated once a day for nine consecutive days.)

Prayer for Generosity of St. Ignatius Loyola

Take, O Lord, all my liberty. Receive my memory, my understanding, and my will. You have given me all that I am and all that I possess. I return it all to You and surrender it to the guidance of Your will. Give me only Your love and Your grace. With these I am rich enough and ask nothing more.

Prayer to Our Lady, Queen of Martyrs

Glorious Queen of Martyrs, to whom the early missionaries of this country were so devoted and from whom they received so many favors, graciously listen to my petitions. Ask your Divine Son to remember all they did for His Glory; remind Him that they preached the Gospel and made His Name known to thousands who had never heard of Him; and then for Him had their apostolic labors crowned by shedding their blood. Exercise your motherly influence as you did at Cana and implore Him to grant me what I ask in this novena, if it be conformable to His Holy Will. Amen.

Prayer in Honor of the North American Martyrs

O God, who by the preaching and blood of Your Sainted Martyrs, Isaac, John, and their companions did consecrate the first fruits of the faith in the vast regions of North America, graciously grant that by their intercession the flourishing harvest of Christians may everywhere and always be increased through Jesus Christ, Our Lord. Amen.

Our Father; Hail Mary

Novena Prayer in Honor of the Martyrs
O God, who did inflame the hearts of Your Blessed Martyrs with an admirable zeal for the salvation of souls, grant me, I beseech You *(mention your request here)*, so that the favors obtained through their intercession may make manifest before all the power and the glory of Your name. Amen.

Prayer for the Canonization
of Blessed Kateri Tekakwitha
O God, who among the many marvels of Your Grace in the New World did cause to blossom on the banks of the Mohawk and of the St. Lawrence the pure and tender Lily, Kateri Tekakwitha, grant we beseech You the favor we beg through her intercession — that this young Lover of Jesus and of His Cross may soon be counted among her saints by the Church and that our hearts may be enkindled with a stronger desire to imitate her innocence and faith. Through the same Christ Our Lord. Amen.

Martyrs Shrine

The Shrine to the North American Martyrs was built in 1885 at the site of a Mohawk village that is believed to be the village of Ossernenon. It was here that St. René Goupil was martyred in 1642 and his body thrown in the nearby ravine. Four years later, St. Isaac Jogues and St. John Lalande were martyred here with their bodies thrown into the Mohawk River in the valley below and their heads impaled on the stockade that surrounded the village.

The main church of the shrine is built in the shape of the Roman Coliseum, symbolic of the early Christian martyrs. The grounds are filled with chapels including one to Blessed Kateri Tekakwitha, who was born here and lived most of her life in nearby Fonda, which is a few miles from Auriesville. Jesuit priests and brothers from the New York province who have continued the work of the North American Martyrs are buried in a cemetery that lies directly behind the final station of the cross.

Shrine of Our Lady of Martyrs
Route 5S and Noeltner Road
Auriesville, NY 12016
Telephone: 518-853-3033
Website: http://klink.net/~jesuit/

CHAPTER 22

St. Elizabeth Ann Seton

Mother and Teacher

History of the Devotion

Elizabeth Bayley was born on August 28, 1774, in New York City to Catherine Charlton and Dr. Richard Bayley. Her parents were devout Episcoplians. When Elizabeth was nineteen, she married William Seton, a rich shipping merchant. They lived in Manhattan where over the course of the next eight years they had five children.

In 1799, William Seton's shipping business was near bankruptcy and his health was failing. Four years later, the couple, taking their eldest child with them, traveled to Italy in hopes that the change in climate would improve William's health. It did not and on December 27, 1803, William died in Italy. Elizabeth was a widow and stranded in a foreign land.

She stayed with the Filicchis, a wealthy Italian family who were devout Catholics. During her grief, Elizabeth found herself drawn to the faith of the Filicchis. When she returned to New York in 1804, she horrified her family and friends by announcing that she had decided to become a Catholic. Elizabeth Ann Seton — a widow, penniless, and with no support from her family — became a Catholic on March 14, 1805.

For several years the young single mother tried a number of occupations in an attempt to support her family. All of them failed. In 1809, she decided to pursue the profession of her father, who had been a professor at Kings College (modern-day Columbia University).

The rector of St. Mary's Seminary in Baltimore informed her that the archbishop of Baltimore was interested in starting a school for girls in the Archdiocese of Baltimore.

Unable to make enough money in New York to support her family, she moved to Baltimore at the invitation of Archbishop John Carroll to establish such a school there. Soon she was joined by other young women and with Elizabeth Ann Seton they formed a new religious community: the Sisters of Charity of St. Joseph's. They founded a school for poor children as well, beginning the parochial school movement in the United States.

In 1812, Archbishop Carroll approved the rule of the new community, which then consisted of eighteen nuns. The newly approved community elected Elizabeth as the superior of the group now known as the Sisters of Charity.

Mother Seton suffered the further loss of two of her daughters who died at a very young age. The pain and grief only seemed to strengthen her deep faith in God.

The community of nuns that she founded at the time of her death on January 4, 1821, has blossomed today into an international community of some twenty-eight thousand Sisters of Charity. Pope Paul VI canonized Mother Seton on September 14, 1975. She is the first native-born American to be canonized.

Novena to
St. Elizabeth Ann Seton

(The following prayers are repeated once a day for nine consecutive days.)

Prayer to the Holy Spirit *(see "Prayers Common to Novenas," p. 252)*

Prayer of St. Elizabeth Ann Seton to God the Father
O Father, the first rule of Our dear Savior's life was to do Your Will. Let His Will of the present moment be the first rule of our daily life and work, with no other desire but for its most full and complete accomplishment. Help us to follow it faithfully, so that doing what You wish we will be pleasing to You. Amen.

Prayer to Our Lord in the Blessed Sacrament
Lord Jesus Christ, truly present in the Blessed Sacrament, make our hearts and souls to know and understand the grace of the Holy Sacrament of the Altar as St. Elizabeth Ann Seton did. Grant us her fervor in adoration, her ardor in communion, and her unceasing desire for eternal union with You. Amen.

Memorare *(see "Prayers Common to Novenas," p. 252)*

Novena Prayer
O Mary, conceived without sin, pray for us who have recourse to you.

Elizabeth Ann Seton, pray for us.
(Mention your request here.)

Lord God, You blessed Elizabeth Ann Seton with gifts of grace as wife and mother, educator and foundress, so that she might spend her life in service to Your people. Through her example and prayers, may we learn to express our love for You in love for our fellow men and women. We ask this through Our Lord Jesus Christ, Your Son, who lives and reigns with You and the Holy Spirit, one God, forever and ever. Amen.

Prayer of St. Elizabeth Ann Seton

Lord Jesus, who was born for us in a stable, lived for us a life of pain and sorrow, and died for us upon a cross; say for us in the hour of death, "Father, forgive," and to Thy Mother, "Behold thy child." Say to us, "This day you shall be with Me in paradise." Dear Savior, leave us not, forsake us not. We thirst for You, Fountain of Living Water. Our days pass quickly along; soon all will be consummated for us. Into Your hands we commend our spirits, now and forever. Amen.

Final Acclamation

Elizabeth Ann Seton, you are a saint for our time.

Elizabeth Ann Seton, you are a woman of faith, for a time of doubt and uncertainty.

Elizabeth Ann Seton, you are a woman of love, for a time of coldness and division.

Elizabeth Ann Seton, you are a woman of hope, for a time of crisis and discouragement.

Intercede for our Church and our country. Amen.

Basilica of the National Shrine of St. Elizabeth Ann Seton

The Shrine of St. Elizabeth Ann Seton is built on the site where Mother Seton spent her life from 1809 until her death in 1821. A visitor center contains a museum with material that illustrates Mother Seton's life and after her death the history of her canonization process.

A large chapel, completed in 1965 in anticipation of Mother Seton's canonization, contains relics of Mother Seton. The chapel was designated a minor basilica in 1991 by Pope John Paul II. The original stone house where Mother Seton founded the Sisters of Charity and the house where she founded the first parochial school are also located on the shrine grounds.

Seton Shrine Center
333 South Seton Avenue
Emmitsburg, MD 21727
Telephone: 301-447-6606
E-mail: office@setonshrine.org
Website: http://www.setonshrine.org/

CHAPTER 23
St. Frances Xavier Cabrini

Patroness of All Immigrants

History of the Devotion

Maria Francesca Cabrini was born on July 15, 1850, the last of the thirteen children of Agostino and Stella Cabrini, in Sant' Angelo Lodigiano, a town in the region of Lombardy, Italy. Her early years were filled with dreams of being a great missionary for Christ like St. Francis Xavier and making the Gospel known to people in faraway places like China. However, the realization of this dream seemed highly improbable due to Maria's frail nature.

In 1868, she obtained her teaching diploma and taught for the next six years near her home. In 1874, Maria joined two other laywomen at the invitation of Father Antonio Serrati in the administration of an orphanage. He wanted Maria to form her fellow workers in the spirit of a religious community. Three years later, Maria took the religious name Xavier (after her hero) and made her religious profession. In 1880, Mother Cabrini founded what would later be known as the Institute of the Missionary Sisters of the Sacred Heart of Jesus.

In an audience with Pope Leo XIII, Mother Cabrini requested that her nuns be allowed to travel to China as missionaries. The pope refused this request but instead asked Mother Cabrini to make New York her order's mission.

In March of 1989, Mother Cabrini arrived in America with six of her nuns. She immediately went to work opening an orphanage and a free school in the Italian-dominated Lower East Side of Manhattan. It was the start of an amazing mission in which Mother Cabrini's visible presence would not only be felt but left across the continent of the United States.

She opened schools not only in New York but also in Philadelphia, New Orleans, Chicago, Denver, Seattle, and Los Angeles. Orphanages and hospitals were opened too. Her work continued to flourish in Italy as well as spreading to France, Spain, Panama, Nicaragua, Argentina, and Brazil. In the sixty-seven years that Mother Cabrini would spend on this earth, a like number of institutions came into existence through her efforts.

Crossing the ocean twenty-five times, she would return from each journey with more nuns anxious to join her missionary efforts. In 1909, Mother Cabrini became a naturalized citizen of the United States of America in a ceremony that took place in Seattle, Washington. In 1910, the Missionary Sisters of the Sacred Heart of Jesus named her superior for life.

Toward the end of her life she purchased land on a mountainside where she hoped to establish a camp for children who lived at a nearby orphanage in Denver that she had also founded. The land was high in the mountains, and professionals looked in vain to find any water on the property. Mother Cabrini, on a visit with her nuns, pointed to a red rock on the property and told them authoritatively that they would find water there. The workers drilled in the unlikely spot and water flowed forth. People continue to flock to the source of the miraculous water to this day.

Mother Cabrini died in Chicago on December 22, 1917. She was buried in New York near the Sacred Heart Orphanage that she had founded. In 1933, her remains were transferred to the Chapel of Mother Cabrini High School in the Bronx, where her body is encased under the main altar of the chapel.

She was beatified twenty-one years later by Pope Pius XI, on November 13, 1938, and the decree of canonization was signed by Pope Pius XII on January 11, 1944, but not promulgated until July 7, 1946, because of World War II. She is the first foreign-born American citizen to be canonized a saint in the U.S. In 1950, Pope Pius XII declared Mother Cabrini "Patroness of All Immigrants."

In 1999, *Chicago Magazine* named St. Frances Xavier Cabrini one of the hundred most influential people of the twentieth century in Chicago. In the same year, Pope John Paul II declared her a model saint for evangelization of the new millennium.

Novena to
St. Frances Xavier Cabrini

(The following prayers are repeated once a day for nine consecutive days.)

Almighty and Eternal Father, Giver of all Gifts, show us Your mercy, and grant, we beseech You, through the merits of Your faithful Servant, St. Frances Xavier Cabrini, that all who invoke her intercession may obtain what they desire according to the good pleasure of Your Holy Will *(mention your request here)*.

O Lord Jesus Christ, Savior of the world, mindful of Your bountiful goodness and love, deign, we implore You, through the tender devotion of St. Frances Xavier Cabrini for Your Sacred Heart, to hear our prayers and grant our petitions.

O God, the Holy Spirit, Comforter of the afflicted, Fountain of Light and Truth, through the ardent zeal of Your humble handmaid, St. Frances Xavier Cabrini, grant us Your all-powerful aid in our necessities, sanctify our souls, and fill our minds with Divine Light that we may see the Holy Will of God in all things.

St. Frances Xavier Cabrini, beloved spouse of the Sacred Heart of Jesus, intercede for us that the favor we ask may be granted.

(Say the following prayers three times each.)
Our Father; Hail Mary; Glory Be

National Shrine of St. Frances Xavier Cabrini

One enters the National Shrine of St. Frances Xavier through the halls of the Columbus Hospital that she founded, an apt testament in and of itself to the fruits of Mother Cabrini's earthly ministry. Walking through bronze doors, one enters a beautiful chapel with vaulted dome. Stained-glass windows representing the mysteries of the Rosary, beautiful travertine marble: all were imported from Florence, Italy, to give the chapel a look of elegance. The main altar contains the sacred relic of Mother Cabrini's right humerus (upper part of the right arm bone). The vaulted ceiling is decorated with paintings by Joseph Ciotti depicting the life of St. Frances from her childhood to her role in heaven as patroness of all immigrants.

A museum off to the right of the sanctuary of the chapel contains many second-class relics of the saint (items used by her during her earthly life). These include her habit, nightgown, eating utensils, shoes, and books. Documents including her birth certificate, last will and testament, naturalization papers, death certificate, and the papal proclamation of her as patroness of all immigrants are also displayed in the museum.

The room, where Mother Cabrini spent the last years of her life and where she died, has been reconstructed to its original form and can be viewed from the right of the museum. The bedroom contains all the original furnishings including the wicker chair where Mother Cabrini was sitting when she died in 1917.

The National Shrine of St. Frances Xavier Cabrini
2520 North Lakeview
Chicago, IL 60614
Telephone: 773-388-7338

CHAPTER 24

St. John Neumann

Bishop of Philadelphia

History of the Devotion

John Nepomucene was born in Prachatitz, Bohemia, on March 28, 1811, the son of Agnes and Philip Neumann. Attracted to religious life from an early age and strongly encouraged by his mother, he entered the seminary at the age of twenty and studied at Budweis and Prague. Due to an abundance of priests serving in his native Bohemia, John was unable to find a bishop to ordain him. He was advised to go to the United States, where there was a great need of priests.

Traveling to New York in 1836, he was ordained a priest for the Archdiocese of New York in June of that same year at old St. Patrick's Cathedral. He was sent to be the pastor of the area around Niagara Falls in New York that was heavily populated by Germans. He opened parishes and several schools (in which he himself was a teacher) in western New York State. In 1840, Father Neumann traveled to Pittsburgh, where he joined the newly formed American branch of the Redemptorists. He became the first member of the congregation to profess vows in the United States, which took place in 1842, in Baltimore. During these years, he served at St. Philomena's in Pittsburgh and St. Alphonsus in Baltimore as well as being elected vice-provincial of the missionary order.

On February 10, 1848, Father Neumann became a naturalized citizen of the United States. Four years later, in 1852, he was consecrated the fourth bishop of Philadelphia. He journeyed throughout his extensive diocese, using every means of travel available to him and using his multilingual gift (he spoke nine languages) to reach his diverse immigrant flock. During his eight years as bishop of Philadelphia, he opened eighty churches and thirty-four schools.

Bishop Neumann had a strong devotion to Jesus' presence in the Blessed Sacrament and established the Forty Hours Devotion throughout his diocese that subsequently spread throughout the United States. He was revered throughout the northeast for his exemplary holiness, self-sacrifice, and constant effort to help his fellow immigrants maintain their Catholic faith in the new land to which they had come.

On January 5, 1860, the bishop collapsed a few blocks from the cathedral and died a short time later. His body was buried in the crypt of St. Peter's Church, the Redemptorist church in Philadelphia.

Devotion to the bishop continued, and numerous miracles were ascribed to his intercession including the healing of a young boy who was dying of cancer and whose miraculous recovery took place after the boy visited the bishop's shrine. This miracle, which the doctors said was scientifically and medically unexplainable, paved the way for Bishop Neumann's canonization by Pope Paul VI on June 19, 1977.

Novena to St. John Neumann

FIRST DAY

O St. John Neumann, obtain for me a lively faith in all the truths that the Holy Roman Catholic Church teaches, together with the divine light to know the vanity of all earthly things, and the hideousness of my sins. Obtain for me also the special favor of *(mention your request here)* that I now ask through your intercession with God.

Let us pray:

O Lord, who on earth both praised and practiced the hidden life, grant that, in these days of pride and outward display, the humble ways of Your servant St. John Neumann may inspire us to imitate Your divine example.

Teach us, O Divine Master, to be like Your servant the holy bishop, intent on pleasing only You and on performing our good actions free from the desire to be seen and glorified by men.

That his holy example may influence an ever-increasing number of souls, grant, O Lord, the favors we ask through his intercession. Amen.

(Say the following prayers three times each.)
Our Father; Hail Mary; Glory Be

SECOND DAY

O St. John Neumann, obtain for me the firm hope of receiving from God, through the merits of Jesus Christ and the intercession of Mary and your prayers the pardon of my sins, final perseverance, and paradise. Obtain for me also the special favor of *(mention your request here)* that I now ask through your intercession with God.

Let us pray:

O Lord, who on earth both praised and practiced the hidden life, grant that, in these days of pride and outward display, the humble ways of Your servant St. John Neumann may inspire us to imitate Your divine example.

Teach us, O Divine Master, to be like Your servant the holy bishop, intent on pleasing only You and on performing our good actions free from the desire to be seen and glorified by men.

That his holy example may influence an ever-increasing number of souls, grant, O Lord, the favors we ask through his intercession. Amen.

(Say the following prayers three times each.)
Our Father; Hail Mary; Glory Be

THIRD DAY

O St. John Neumann, obtain for me an ardent love of God that will detach me from the love of created things and from myself, to love Him alone and to spend myself for His glory. Obtain for me also the special favor of *(mention your request here)* that I now ask through your intercession with God.

Let us pray:

O Lord, who on earth both praised and practiced the hidden life, grant that, in these days of pride and outward display, the humble ways of Your servant St. John Neumann may inspire us to imitate Your divine example.

Teach us, O Divine Master, to be like Your servant the holy bishop, intent on pleasing only You and on performing our good actions free from the desire to be seen and glorified by men.

That his holy example may influence an ever-increasing number of souls, grant, O Lord, the favors we ask through his intercession. Amen.

(Say the following prayers three times each.)
Our Father; Hail Mary; Glory Be

FOURTH DAY

O St. John Neumann, obtain for me perfect resignation to the will of God, that I may accept in peace, sufferings, contempt, persecutions, loss of goods, and reputation, and finally death itself. Obtain for me also the special favor of *(mention your request here)* that I now ask through your intercession with God.

Let us pray:
O Lord, who on earth both praised and practiced the hidden life, grant that, in these days of pride and outward display, the humble ways of Your servant St. John Neumann may inspire us to imitate Your divine example.

Teach us, O Divine Master, to be like Your servant the holy bishop, intent on pleasing only You and on performing our good actions free from the desire to be seen and glorified by men.

That his holy example may influence an ever-increasing number of souls, grant, O Lord, the favors we ask through his intercession. Amen.

(Say the following prayers three times each.)
Our Father; Hail Mary; Glory Be

FIFTH DAY

O St. John Neumann, obtain for me a heartfelt sorrow for my sins, that I may never cease to weep over the displeasure I have given my God. Obtain for me also the special favor of *(mention your request here)* that I now ask through your intercession with God.

Let us pray:

O Lord, who on earth both praised and practiced the hidden life, grant that, in these days of pride and outward display, the humble ways of Your servant St. John Neumann may inspire us to imitate Your divine example.

Teach us, O Divine Master, to be like Your servant the holy bishop, intent on pleasing only You and on performing our good actions free from the desire to be seen and glorified by men.

That his holy example may influence an ever-increasing number of souls, grant, O Lord, the favors we ask through his intercession. Amen.

(Say the following prayers three times each.)
Our Father; Hail Mary; Glory Be

SIXTH DAY

O St. John Neumann, obtain for me a true love of my neighbor that will make me do good even to those who have offended me. Obtain for me also the special favor of *(mention your request here)* that I now ask through your intercession with God.

Let us pray:

O Lord, who on earth both praised and practiced the hidden life, grant that, in these days of pride and outward display, the humble ways of Your servant St. John Neumann may inspire us to imitate Your divine example.

Teach us, O Divine Master, to be like Your servant the holy bishop, intent on pleasing only You and on performing our good actions free from the desire to be seen and glorified by men.

That his holy example may influence an ever-increasing number of souls, grant, O Lord, the favors we ask through his intercession. Amen.

(Say the following prayers three times each.)
Our Father; Hail Mary; Glory Be

SEVENTH DAY

O St. John Neumann, obtain for me the virtue of holy purity and the help required to resist impure temptations by invoking the holy names of Jesus and Mary. Obtain for me also the special favor of *(mention your request here)* that I now ask through your intercession with God.

Let us pray:

O Lord, who on earth both praised and practiced the hidden life, grant that, in these days of pride and outward display, the humble ways of Your servant St. John Neumann may inspire us to imitate Your divine example.

Teach us, O Divine Master, to be like Your servant the

holy bishop, intent on pleasing only You and on performing our good actions free from the desire to be seen and glorified by men.

That his holy example may influence an ever-increasing number of souls, grant, O Lord, the favors we ask through his intercession. Amen.

(Say the following prayers three times each.)
Our Father; Hail Mary; Glory Be

EIGHTH DAY

O St. John Neumann, obtain for me a tender devotion to the Passion of Jesus Christ, to the Blessed Sacrament, and to my dear Mother Mary. Obtain for me also the special favor of *(mention your request here)* that I now ask through your intercession with God.

Let us pray:
O Lord, who on earth both praised and practiced the hidden life, grant that, in these days of pride and outward display, the humble ways of Your servant St. John Neumann may inspire us to imitate Your divine example.

Teach us, O Divine Master, to be like Your servant the holy bishop, intent on pleasing only You and on performing our good actions free from the desire to be seen and glorified by men.

That his holy example may influence an ever-increasing number of souls, grant, O Lord, the favors we ask through his intercession. Amen.

(Say the following prayers three times each.)
Our Father; Hail Mary; Glory Be

NINTH DAY

O St. John Neumann, obtain for me above all the grace of final perseverance and the grace always to pray for it, especially in time of temptation and at the hour of death. Obtain for me also the special favor of *(mention your request here)* that I now ask through your intercession with God.

Let us pray:

O Lord, who on earth both praised and practiced the hidden life, grant that, in these days of pride and outward display, the humble ways of Your servant St. John Neumann may inspire us to imitate Your divine example.

Teach us, O Divine Master, to be like Your servant the holy bishop, intent on pleasing only You and on performing our good actions free from the desire to be seen and glorified by men.

That his holy example may influence an ever-increasing number of souls, grant, O Lord, the favors we ask through his intercession. Amen.

Closing Novena Prayer

O my God, I adore Your infinite Majesty with all the powers of my soul. I thank You for the graces and gifts which You bestowed upon Your faithful servant, St. John Neumann. I ask You to glorify him also on earth. For this end I beseech You to grant me the favor which I humbly ask from Your Fatherly mercy. Amen.

(Say the following prayers three times each.)
Our Father; Hail Mary; Glory Be

National Shrine
of St. John Neumann

St. John Neumann's body lies in repose under the main altar of the shrine in the crypt of St. Peter's Church. A wax mask covers the saint's face. People visit from all around the world to pray before the saint's remains and to implore his intercession. The shrine is staffed by the Redemptorists, the congregation that St. John Neumann had joined in 1842 as the first priest to join the American branch.

National Shrine of St. John Neumann
1019 North Fifth Street
Philadelphia, PA 19123
Telephone: 215-627-3080
E-mail: neumann@philanet.com
Website: http://www.stjohnneumann.org/

CHAPTER 25

Blessed Katharine Drexel

Evangelist to People of Color

History of the Devotion

Katharine Mary Drexel was born on November 26, 1858, to Hannah and Francis Drexel in Philadelphia. Her mother died about five weeks after her birth. Her father was very wealthy and a business partner of banker J. P. Morgan. He married Emma Bouvier, and together they continued what Hannah had begun: raising Katharine and her sister in the Catholic faith.

Her stepmother set an early example for the young Katharine that was to instill a value of helping others and using the wealth that her family possessed for the good of others. Three afternoons of every week Emma would open the doors of the family household and distribute food, clothing, and money to those in need.

When Katharine turned twenty-five, her stepmother died; two years later, in 1885, her father died, leaving the three Drexel daughters a fortune in trust to divide among themselves. Around this time two priests visited Katharine and made her aware of the plight of the Native Americans in the Dakotas. They told her the government was cutting off funding of the schools in their missions and they needed help. She immediately wrote a check to help them.

A short while after this episode, in a private audience with Pope Leo XIII she boldly asked the Holy Father to send priests to the Indians of the United States. The pope's response to her was, "Why not, my child, yourself become a missionary?" This seemed to act as a confirmation of a vocation that she had been trying to discern since she was fourteen.

In 1889, Katharine made headlines in a Philadelphia paper when she entered a convent. She remained with the Sisters of Mercy for two years for training in religious life, then founded in 1891 a new community whose members would minister to Native and African Americans. She called her community the Sisters of the Blessed Sacrament.

The first community of nuns was sent to Santa Fe, New Mexico, to start a school for the Native American children there. Soon other schools were opened in the West and in the rural south for African Americans. She opened Xavier University in New Orleans, the first black Catholic university. These efforts were not welcomed by some of the local populace.

Mother Drexel had a heart attack in 1935 and spent the

last twenty years of her life in a more contemplative manner. Through her prayers and the work of her nuns the fight continued for the civil rights of the people who were denied those rights because of the color of their skin. She died on March 3, 1955.

Pope John Paul II beatified Mother Drexel in 1988, and the Vatican is investigating a miracle needed for her canonization.

Novena to Blessed Katharine Drexel

(The following prayer is repeated once a day for nine consecutive days.)

God of Love, come to our assistance; open our hearts and our minds to hear the voice of the Spirit speaking within us. Ever loving God, You called Blessed Katharine Drexel to share the message of the Gospel and the life of the Eucharist with the poor oppressed among Native and African American peoples. Through her intercession, may we grow in faith and love that will enable us to be united as brothers and sisters in You.

In particular we ask *(mention your request here)*.

May Your servant Katharine Drexel soon be declared a saint by the Church so that You may be glorified and we may strive for greater unity, justice, and peace. We pray this through Jesus Christ, Our Lord. Amen.

Shrine of Blessed Katharine Drexel

The Shrine of Blessed Katharine Drexel, who is expected to soon be St. Katharine, is located in the motherhouse of the Sisters of the Blessed Sacrament, the community of nuns she founded in 1891. Her tomb is located beneath the motherhouse chapel, and various artifacts tell the story of Mother Drexel's love and dedication to Native and African American people.

Shrine of Blessed Katharine Drexel
1663 Bristol Pike
Bensalem, PA 19020-8502
Telephone: 215-639-7878
E-mail: sbs@libertynet.org
Website: http://www.katharinedrexel.org/

Part 7

Novena for the Holy Souls

"Let us not hesitate to help those who have died
and to offer our prayers for them."

CATECHISM OF THE CATHOLIC CHURCH, NO. 1032

CHAPTER 26

St. Odilo

Patron of the
Poor Souls in Purgatory

History of the Devotion

At the age of twenty-nine, Odilo was made coadjutor to the abbot who gave him the monastic habit at the Benedictine monastery at Cluny. Three years later, the abbot died and Odilo succeeded him as abbot. During his reign as abbot, a great famine spread throughout France, and Abbot Odilo ordered some of the sacred vessels that were made of gold to be melted down so that food could be purchased for the poor.

Besides his charitable works and his efforts in seeing that churches were places of refuge for souls escaping the ravages of war, Odilo's lasting legacy is the Feast of All Souls. He instituted an annual day, November 2, to be celebrated by all the monasteries that followed the Cluny reforms of the Benedictine rule. The monks were to remember all the deceased members of their community and their benefactors. The commemoration was to be done not only by reciting prayers but also by giving alms and making personal sacrifices.

Odilo suffered many diseases during the last five years of his life. He died while lying on the ground on sackcloth and ashes at the priory at Souvigny, where he had been making a monastic visitation. He was eighty-seven and had been abbot at Cluny for fifty-six years.

Novena for the Poor Souls

FIRST DAY

O Lord, hear my prayer and let my cry come to You.

Let us pray:

God, the Creator and Redeemer of all the faithful, grant to the souls of Your servants and handmaids the remission of all their sins, that through our sincere prayers they may obtain the pardon they have always desired. Through Christ our Lord. Amen.

Lord God, by the Precious Blood which Your divine Son, Jesus, shed in the garden, deliver the souls in purgatory, especially those souls who are the most forsaken of all. Bring them into Your glory, where they may praise and bless You forever. Amen.

Our Father; Hail Mary

Eternal rest grant unto them, O Lord, and let perpetual light shine upon them.

May they rest in peace. Amen.

May their souls and the souls of all the faithful departed, through the mercy of God, rest in peace. Amen.

SECOND DAY

O Lord, hear my prayer and let my cry come to You.

Let us pray:

God, the Creator and Redeemer of all the faithful, grant to the souls of Your servants and handmaids the remission of all their sins, that through our sincere prayers they may obtain the pardon they have always desired. Through Christ our Lord. Amen.

Lord God, by the Precious Blood which your divine Son, Jesus, shed in His cruel scourging, deliver the souls in purgatory and among them those souls who are nearest to sharing Your glory that they may fully praise and bless You forever. Amen.

Our Father; Hail Mary

Eternal rest grant unto them, O Lord, and let perpetual light shine upon them.

May they rest in peace. Amen.

May their souls and the souls of all the faithful departed, through the mercy of God, rest in peace. Amen.

THIRD DAY

O Lord, hear my prayer and let my cry come to You.

Let us pray:

God, the Creator and Redeemer of all the faithful, grant to the souls of Your servants and handmaids the remission of all their sins, that through our sincere prayers they may obtain the pardon they have always desired. Through Christ our Lord. Amen.

Lord God, by the Precious Blood of Your divine Son, Jesus, which was shed in His bitter crowning with thorns, deliver the souls in purgatory, and among them those souls who are in greatest need of our prayers, in order that they may not long be delayed in praising You fully in Your glory and blessing You forever. Amen.

Our Father; Hail Mary

Eternal rest grant unto them, O Lord, and let perpetual light shine upon them.

May they rest in peace. Amen.

May their souls and the souls of all the faithful departed, through the mercy of God, rest in peace. Amen.

FOURTH DAY

O Lord, hear my prayer and let my cry come to You.

Let us pray:

God, the Creator and Redeemer of all the faithful, grant to the souls of Your servants and handmaids the remission of all their sins, that through our sincere prayers they may obtain the pardon they have always desired. Through Christ our Lord. Amen.

Lord God, by the Precious Blood of Your divine Son, Jesus, which was shed in the streets of Jerusalem while He carried the Cross, deliver the souls in purgatory, especially those who are richest in merits in Your sight, so that when they have attained the high place to which they are destined, they may praise You triumphantly and bless You forever. Amen.

Our Father; Hail Mary

Eternal rest grant unto them, O Lord, and let perpetual light shine upon them.

May they rest in peace. Amen.

May their souls and the souls of all the faithful departed, through the mercy of God, rest in peace. Amen.

FIFTH DAY

O Lord, hear my prayer and let my cry come to You.

Let us pray:

God, the Creator and Redeemer of all the faithful, grant to the souls of Your servants and handmaids the remission of all their sins, that through our sincere prayers they may obtain the pardon they have always desired. Through Christ our Lord. Amen.

Lord God, by the Precious Body and Blood of Your divine Son, Jesus, which on the night before His passion He gave to His beloved Apostles and willed to His holy Church as a perpetual sacrifice and spiritual nourishment, deliver the souls in purgatory. Most of all, deliver those who were devoted to the mystery of the Eucharist that they may praise You together with Your divine Son and the Holy Spirit in Your glory forever. Amen.

Our Father; Hail Mary

Eternal rest grant unto them, O Lord, and let perpetual light shine upon them.

May they rest in peace. Amen.

May their souls and the souls of all the faithful departed, through the mercy of God, rest in peace. Amen.

SIXTH DAY

O Lord, hear my prayer and let my cry come to You.

Let us pray:

God, the Creator and Redeemer of all the faithful, grant to the souls of Your servants and handmaids the remission of all their sins, that through our sincere prayers they may obtain the pardon they have always desired. Through Christ our Lord. Amen.

Lord God, by the Precious Blood which Jesus, Your divine Son, shed upon the Cross this day, deliver the souls in purgatory, particularly those souls nearest to me and for whom I should pray, that they may come quickly into Your glory to praise and bless You forever. Amen.

Our Father; Hail Mary

Eternal rest grant unto them, O Lord, and let perpetual light shine upon them.

May they rest in peace. Amen.

May their souls and the souls of all the faithful departed, through the mercy of God, rest in peace. Amen.

SEVENTH DAY

O Lord, hear my prayer and let my cry come to You.

Let us pray:

God, the Creator and Redeemer of all the faithful, grant to the souls of Your servants and handmaids the remission of all their sins, that through our sincere prayers they may obtain the pardon they have always desired. Through Christ our Lord. Amen.

Lord God, by the Precious Blood which came forth from the sacred side of Your divine Son, Jesus, in the presence and to the great sorrow of His holy Mother, deliver the souls in purgatory, especially those souls most devoted to this noble Lady, that they may come quickly into Your glory, to praise You with her forever. Amen.

Our Father; Hail Mary

Eternal rest grant unto them, O Lord, and let perpetual light shine upon them.

May they rest in peace. Amen.

May their souls and the souls of all the faithful departed, through the mercy of God, rest in peace. Amen.

EIGHTH DAY

O Lord, hear my prayer and let my cry come to You.

Let us pray:

God, the Creator and Redeemer of all the faithful, grant to the souls of Your servants and handmaids the remission of all their sins, that through our sincere prayers they may obtain the pardon they have always desired. Through Christ our Lord. Amen.

Lord God, by the Precious Blood which Your divine Son, Jesus, shed on the Cross, deliver the souls in purgatory, especially those souls who were consecrated to You in earthly life. Bring them into Your glory, where they may praise and bless You forever. Amen.

Our Father; Hail Mary

Eternal rest grant unto them, O Lord, and let perpetual light shine upon them.

May they rest in peace. Amen.

May their souls and the souls of all the faithful departed, through the mercy of God, rest in peace. Amen.

NINTH DAY

O Lord, hear my prayer and let my cry come to You.

Let us pray:

God, the Creator and Redeemer of all the faithful, grant to the souls of Your servants and handmaids the remission of all their sins, that through our sincere prayers they may obtain the pardon they have always desired. Through Christ our Lord. Amen.

Lord God, by the Precious Blood which Your divine Son, Jesus, left as a memorial of His Passion, Death, and Resurrection, deliver the souls in purgatory, especially those souls we have commended to You during the course of this novena. Bring them into Your glory, where they may praise and bless You forever. Amen.

Our Father; Hail Mary

Eternal rest grant unto them, O Lord, and let perpetual light shine upon them.

May they rest in peace. Amen.

May their souls and the souls of all the faithful departed, through the mercy of God, rest in peace. Amen.

Adapted from the *Prayer Manual* of the Josephite Fathers and Brothers, Baltimore, Maryland; reprinted with permission.

Shrine of the Poor Souls

The Shrine of the Poor Souls is located at a side altar in the parish church of St. Odilo in Berwyn, Illinois, a suburb of Chicago. The shrine itself centers on a wood carving showing the Blessed Virgin Mary interceding for the souls in torment who reach upward toward heaven, their final reward now in sight. The image portrays that the souls of those who have gone before us have need of our prayers so that when they have completed their heavenly journey they may in turn pray for us.

St. Odilo's
23rd and East Avenue
Berwyn, IL 60402-2499
Telephone: 708-484-2161

Prayers Common to Novenas

The Sign of the Cross
In the name of the Father, and of the Son, and of the Holy Spirit. Amen.

Our Father
Our Father, who art in heaven; hallowed be thy name; thy kingdom come; thy will be done, on earth as it is in heaven. Give us this day our daily bread and forgive us our trespasses as we forgive those who trespass against us. Lead us not into temptation but deliver us from evil. Amen.

Hail Mary
Hail, Mary, full of grace, the Lord is with you. Blessed are you among women, and blessed is the fruit of your womb, Jesus. Holy Mary, Mother of God, pray for us sinners, now and at the hour of our death. Amen.

Glory Be
Glory be to the Father, and to the Son, and to the Holy Spirit. As it was in the beginning, is now, and ever shall be world without end. Amen.

Apostles' Creed
I believe in God, the Father almighty, Creator of heaven and earth. I believe in Jesus Christ, his only Son, our Lord. He was conceived by the Holy Spirit and born of the Virgin Mary. He suffered under Pontius Pilate, was crucified, died, and was buried. He descended into hell. The third day he rose again. He ascended into heaven and is seated at the right hand of the Father. He will come again to judge the living and the dead. I believe in the Holy Spirit, the holy catholic

Church, the communion of saints, the forgiveness of sins, the resurrection of the body, and life everlasting. Amen.

Prayer to the Holy Spirit

Come, Holy Spirit, fill the hearts of your faithful and kindle in them the fire of your love. Send forth your Spirit, and they shall be created. And you shall renew the face of the earth.

Let us pray:

O God, who instruct the hearts of the faithful by the light of the Holy Spirit, grant us in the same spirit to savor what is right, and always to rejoice in his consolation. Through Jesus Christ our Lord. Amen.

Memorare

Remember, O most gracious Virgin Mary, that never was it known that anyone who fled to your protection, implored your help, or sought your intercession, was left unaided. Inspired by this confidence, I fly unto you, O Virgin of virgins, my Mother. To you do I come, before you I stand, sinful and sorrowful. O Mother of the Word Incarnate, despise not my petitions, but in your mercy hear and answer me. Amen.

About the Author

Michael Dubruiel holds a master's degree in Christian Spirituality from Creighton University in Omaha, Nebraska.

He has written for a number of Catholic publications and coauthored with Amy Welborn the *Biblical Way of the Cross*, which was published in 1994 by Ave Maria Press.